MW01624278

HOW **SUCCESSFUL PEOPLE** IMPROVE THEIR MORNING ROUTINE, DAILY HABITS AND **GUARANTEE** THEMSELVES RESULTS

John Lamerton

Let's Tell Your Story Publishing
London

COPYRIGHT

Title: Routine Machine: How successful people improve their morning routine, daily habits and guarantee themselves results

First published in 2019

Address: Let's Tell Your Story Publishing, 5 Century Court, Tolpits Lane, Watford, UK WD18 9RS

ISBN: 978-1-910600-27-6 (Paperback version)

`

ROUTINE
/RU:ˈTI:N/

noun:
A sequence of actions regularly followed.

adjective:
Performed as part of a regular procedure rather than for a special reason.

MACHINE
/MƏˈΣI:N/

noun:
An apparatus using mechanical power and having several parts, each with a definite function and together performing a particular task.

- Any device that transmits a force or directs its application.
- An efficient and well-organised group of powerful people.
- A person who acts with the mechanical efficiency of a machine.

For Jack and Harry.

CONTENTS

ACKNOWLEDGEMENTS

Ah, the difficult second book! That awkward place where I think I have enough to say on a new topic that wasn't covered in my first one and where I may finally, after 20 years, be "found out".

Nothing encapsulates the author's "difficult second book" dilemma better than trying to come up with a page of acknowledgements. I could, of course, just thank the same people again (they do still exist, and I'm still eternally grateful to them), but anyone who's read *'Big Ideas... for Small Businesses'* would immediately be saying to themselves, "Hang on, I read all this in his last book! Has he *nothing* new to say?"

If I've learned anything as an author, it's not to annoy people on page one of your book, so I'll keep the acknowledgements a) brief, and b) different from the first book.

To those I thanked previously, thank you once again for everything that you do and everything that you've done for me.

I get to stand on stage and take all the credit for this book, but without a strong team behind me, I'd be waving a tiny pamphlet with a few hand-scribbled notes, full of spelling mistakes and grammatical errors. It would look crap. And it would *be* crap.

To those I didn't thank first time around but who thought that I *should* have done, what can I say? Any omission was purely unintentional, and I really do appreciate all the support and love that I've had over the years.

I know how lucky I am. In an alternate universe, I may still be a civil servant; clock-watching all day and wishing away the hours, weeks, months and years until retirement. But I found another way. And I was helped along the way by a cast of thousands.

No matter who you are, however small or insignificant a part you think you might have played, I assure you that if we've interacted at all in the last 20 years then you've influenced me in some way and helped shape the person I am today.

A lot of credit has to go to Greg Fidgeon for his amazing editing skills. He's able to make my writing pretty much readable. The number of times he tweaked my work and I made a note to challenge him, but then thought: "No, he's right – the bastard!"

Thanks, once again, to Lee Hallett from LCG Design for the fantastic cover artwork. You've really encapsulated all that it takes to become a Routine Machine in the design, while also having some clear nods to "that first book".

If this book is any good (and I'll let you be the judge of that), that's due to the whip-cracking, arse-kicking ability of Colette Mason from Let's Tell Your Story Publishing. Colette won't let me get away with anything that's just "good enough" (and believe me, my natural tendency is to do the bare minimum of work). And it's thanks to Colette that this entire project took less than eight months from bashing out my first few words on a blank Google Doc to launching the finished article.

And, finally, to those I've never met – hello! I truly hope you enjoy reading the next few hundred pages of my semi-literate ramblings. I'd love to hear from you if this book inspires or helps you in any way. Just drop me a line at john@bigidea.co.uk.

Let's do this, shall we?

INTRODUCTION

> *"You'll never change your life until you change something you do daily. The secret of your success is found in your daily routine."*
>
> *John C Maxwell*

The Monkey, the Human, and the Computer

We are all routine machines.

Your brain is one of the most efficient machines known to Man; capable of running every single function of the human body for a hundred years or more without so much as a day off. It works while you sleep. It's working right now. It can heal bones, grow hair, fight infections and win you points at your local pub quiz.

And a great deal of it runs on routine.

You don't have to *consciously* remember to breathe, do you? Nobody thinks, "It's been a while since I blinked, I'd better have a good blink now."

Thankfully, tasks like reminding the heart to pump blood all around the body are not manual ones that we humans have to worry about 60 to 100 times per minute.

The human brain is a complex machine and one that has evolved over a couple of hundred-thousand years. Granted, we are no longer living in caves, bashing each other over the head with clubs and grunting at each other, but nor are we too dissimilar from our caveman and cavewoman ancestors when it comes to certain parts of the brain anatomy.

Let's do some pretty basic brain surgery, shall we?

In his 2012 book *'The Chimp Paradox'*, Professor Steve Peters – a psychiatrist who works with elite athletes including most famously the British Cycling team – explains in plain English (that even I could understand) how the human brain works.

There are three psychological parts of the brain, known as the frontal lobe, the limbic system and the parietal. How these three parts team up and work together (or, in many cases, don't) determines your thoughts, emotions and feelings.

THE HUMAN

The frontal lobe is responsible for your logical and rational thinking. Every time you solve a crossword, start pondering difficult decisions or try to make a judgement call based on facts you are using the frontal lobe.

This part of the brain wants to help others, feel fulfilled, and be happy and content. It acts according to the programming of what you believe to be right or wrong and what's important to you.

This is the human part of the brain.

THE MONKEY

The limbic system is the emotional part of the brain. It works completely separately from the Human and offers emotion-based responses to situations.

It has one primary role – to keep you alive.

It will alert you to any danger that it perceives in the area. Our ancestors found this very useful when they came face-to-face with a sabre-toothed tiger. The "fight or flight" response generated by the limbic system literally saved their lives.

This part of the brain works four times quicker than the Human, which is why you may find yourself immediately reacting emotionally to situations and later regretting your actions. When you experience feelings of fear, anger, paranoia or despair, it'll be the limbic system that's generating those feelings.

Seeing threats everywhere, making knee-jerk emotional decisions, and shouting and screaming at you to enter "fight or flight" mode?

That'll be the monkey part of the brain.

THE COMPUTER

The final area that we'll look at is the Computer. This is a storage area spread throughout the entire brain and is full of the thoughts, behaviours and patterns that have been programmed into it over the years.

Both the Human and the Monkey have access to it, and both are able to program the Computer. The Computer's job is to provide an automatic response for any given request.

The Computer can operate much faster than either the Human or the Monkey. It can react five times faster than the Monkey and up to 20 times the speed of the Human.

When the Monkey touches fire for the first time, he programs the Computer to remember in future that fire is hot and fire is dangerous. Next time you see fire, the Computer automatically alerts you not to get too close without the Monkey needing to get involved.

When you clean your teeth, you don't need to consciously think about how to do it. The Human programmed the Computer with the instructions, the *routine*, decades ago.

And every time you pick up your toothbrush, the Computer runs that program. The Human and the Monkey can both remain fast asleep, tucked up in their beds.

As you go through your daily life and start interacting with the world at large, the three parts of your brain all receive and interpret the information all around you.

First, the Computer will check its files to see if there's a program already available to re-run. If there is, the Human and the Monkey don't get involved. The Computer runs the program and you act on autopilot.

If the Computer *doesn't* find an existing program, then it shuts down and hands control over how to react to the Human and the Monkey.

The Human will evaluate the facts and figures. It will consider what it knows to be true, play through likely outcomes and make a balanced decision that will give the optimum result.

The Monkey will use its feelings, emotions and first impressions to avoid you getting killed.

If you listen to the Monkey, you can end up making knee-jerk reactions, incorrect assumptions and freezing due to paralysing fear. The Monkey doesn't need to work on logic or reason, meaning it can work four times faster than the Human, so the Monkey will often give you "the answer" first.

The Human will also give you an answer, but this will take longer and will be more considered. The Human wants to know all the facts and all the possible outcomes. He (or she) wants to check all the data held in the Computer for relevant cases like this in order to make a considered decision based on fact.

If you listen to the Monkey and act on the Monkey's advice, the Monkey will program the Computer.

If you listen to the Human and act on the Human's advice, the Human gets to program the Computer.

During the course of this book, we're going to ask the Monkey to sit quietly in the corner while the Human and I have a conversation. We're going to ask the Human to add a couple of new programs to the Computer and maybe tweak a little bit of code on some of the existing programs.

Now, the Monkey isn't going to like this and is probably going to squawk and shriek. The Monkey is going to feel threatened by somebody opening up *their* computer programs and changing their code.

Given infinite time, a thousand monkeys with a thousand typewriters may eventually write the entire works of Shakespeare. But that's not a good reason to leave your Monkey in charge of your Computer. It's time to let the Human have a go.

I'm not the special one

This is the part of the book where you get to learn a little bit about me, where I get to big myself up and tell you why you should listen to me. This is where I tell you why I'm the expert in my field and how your life would be so much better if you'd just listen to what I've got to say over the next few hundred pages.

But here's the problem: I'm nothing special.

I'm just a normal bloke from Plymouth, who's done quite well in business. I don't have magic genes and I wasn't born with a silver spoon in my mouth. My dad was an electrician and my mum worked in a sewing factory. I'm not particularly academic. I left school at 16 and pursued a career as a civil servant (a job I ultimately grew to hate).

I haven't always made good decisions. I used to be five stone overweight, and I used to smoke and drink too much. I nearly bankrupted myself in 2006. I've missed hundreds of "golden opportunities" that each could have made me a millionaire many times over, and I've gone into partnerships and business plans that have fallen flat on their face, time and time again.

I used to think the answer to my prayers was simply working harder – that if I somehow put in more work, pulled another all-nighter and just did a few more 100-hour weeks then something would happen and some magic event would suddenly come along and change things.

So, based on all that, why the hell would you listen to me?

Because, *despite* all that, I have been successful. I've made millions of pounds, despite making nearly as many mistakes. Despite leaving school at 16, I'm now a best-selling author.

When I first started out, I knew nothing about business (my first company was an internet marketing firm, which I started after reading *'Internet Marketing for Dummies'* – true story!), yet I've now been involved in more than 60 small businesses. And now hundreds of small business owners have joined our group coaching club, the One Percent Club.

Everything I now own, everything I have in my life right now – it all started with £100. And it wasn't even *my* £100. That was just the size of my overdraft. That's where I started. You may be there or thereabouts yourself, too. You may be worse off or you may be further along the journey. But wherever you are right now, I can honestly say, hand on heart, that if you follow the principles laid out in this book and allow the "hill of time" to "grow your snowball" (those terms will make a lot more sense in a few chapters), you will be amazed by the progress you can make and how easy it appeared given the benefit of hindsight.

I don't have all the answers and I'm not going to pretend I do. What I do have is a simple, practical way to grow a business, to grow wealth, to get healthier, to develop as a human being and to become the person you're truly capable of being without working yourself into the ground. If working harder were the answer, then everybody who works hard would be a multi-millionaire. But take a look around you. You don't need to look far to see people working their arses off and still not getting where they want to be.

Becoming a Routine Machine is not about working hard, it's about doing things differently. Not necessarily the big things either, but a culmination of lots of small tweaks. If you want something different to what you already have then you're going to need to do something different to what you've already been doing. Every single day. Without fail. Routinely.

This book will help you make those small, seemingly insignificant changes that will compound over time to truly change your life. It has worked for me and I'm just a normal bloke from Plymouth. If I can do it, why the hell can't you?

Enter the King of Routine

As part of the marketing push for my first book *'Big Ideas... for Small Businesses,'* I did rather a lot of PR work. I gave talks to rooms full of people from the local Rotary Club to the Federation of Small Businesses. I did Facebook Lives with the local newspaper and became a regular on BBC Radio Devon.

I was also interviewed on some podcasts; talking about everything from my views on lifestyle businesses, how I juggle parenting with growing a business empire and where I feel most small businesses go wrong with their marketing. I turned into a proper media whore and if you had a podcast with more than about three listeners, then I probably appeared as a guest on your show.

One of the biggest I appeared on was *'The ONE Thing',* which is among the top five per cent of podcasts in the world. Considering there are more than half a million active podcasts at the time of writing, that's quite some achievement.

I'd read Gary Keller's book *'The ONE Thing'* several times over the years and it had a profound impact on me, so I was unbelievably excited to appear on the podcast and talk about how I'd applied its principles in my business and my life. I was also extremely nervous.

Now, I can perform a 45-minute talk in front of a room full of strangers, no problem. Go live on Facebook to thousands of people? Easy. Chat live on BBC Radio with tens of thousands of people listening to your every word? Piece of cake. But pre-record a 30-minute podcast episode talking about my life to one of my heroes? Well, this is where my "imposter syndrome" kicked in. This was where I no longer felt like the successful businessman telling the world how he did it. This is where I felt like a lost little boy, who didn't belong on this platform.

Why the hell would one of the top podcasts in the world, whose other guests have included inspirational people like Angela Duckworth, Dave Asprey, Hal Elrod, Jocko Willink, and Cal Newport, be interested in little old me?

Their previous episodes include such titles as 'Seeking guidance from a billionaire', 'How billionaires set goals' and 'The mindset behind a billion-dollar company'. What were their listeners going to think when they heard this bloke from the South West of England, whose greatest achievement was being able to flip 43 beer mats at the same time and whose biggest claim to fame is that he once had a wee next to the snooker player Jimmy White?

I've honestly never been so nervous when recording an interview. I was on edge for the entire time I chatted with host Geoff Woods. I spoke too fast, didn't get enough oxygen in and certainly did not bring the best version of me to the episode. I went on the show to plug my book, yet I barely even mentioned it as I felt that I truly wasn't worthy of appearing on the show.

"These people probably don't want to listen to me. Why the hell would they want to read my book?"

That was my thinking at the time.

It didn't help that The ONE Thing was by far the most professional setup I'd encountered while recording podcast interviews. Whereas just about every other host would turn on the microphones and record a 40-minute chat, The ONE Thing grilled me for 20 minutes the day before recording just to plan what we would talk about during the interview. And on the day of recording, they edited live as we were talking.

I reeled off my famous "Alan Sugar story" (the moment it all changed for me and I became an advocate of lifestyle businesses), which is normally met with amazement, excitement and acts as a real conversation starter. But on The ONE Thing podcast, I was met with the following response: "Hmm."

That was followed by three or four seconds of silence. Cue my confidence dipping even lower. I'd just given them my best story – the one that always gets audiences nodding their heads and joining me on the journey – and it fell flat on its face.

"You talked a bit too much there, John. Can we go again, and let me come in after a few sentences?"

"Hmm."

"I'm not sure that worked."

"Hmm."

Lots of instant feedback, but not the sort I wanted! And then Geoff asked me a question that I wasn't expecting: "Where are you still struggling with the ONE thing?"

The first thing that popped into my head was the way I described myself in every press release I put out for my first book, the way I announced myself every time I went on stage, and how I was introduced every time I went on the radio or did any interviews.

"John Lamerton is a lazy entrepreneur and investor."

I'd fully embraced the "lazy" title. That was a conscious choice, but I was also very much aware that I was using a negative word to describe myself. Geoff went on to do some live coaching around the "lazy" theme and got me to reframe myself as an "effective entrepreneur" on the live call.

During the interview, we talked a lot about how I use routine to achieve so much, how I live and die by my planner, how if it isn't in my calendar it doesn't exist and how doing the same thing every day, every week, every month over a number of years has delivered me success. Not success in the "billionaire" sense, but success for me. I have an ambitious lifestyle business that delivers on my ideal job description – to do *what* I want, *when* I want, *where* I want, *how* I want, *if* I want.

We talked about how there was no massive turning point. No single thing that I did that made all the difference. It was simply years and years of doing the right things day-in, day-out. Routinely.

We talked about how protective I am over my daily routines and how I refuse to let the wrong things get in the way of my doing the right things every single day. Of how much it annoys me when stuff does get in the way and stops me from following my usual routine. And of how quickly I get back on the horse and start following the routine again from the very next opportunity.

After we'd finished recording the episode, Geoff and I stayed on the line and chatted for a few minutes. He said he was glad to have a "normal person" on the show as he felt it would resonate with the audience because they would feel capable of achieving what I have achieved just by doing what I have done. While Tony Robbins is undoubtedly inspirational, you can't help but feel a level of disconnect due to the huge gulf between where you are right now and the guy worth nearly half a billion dollars and with his own Netflix documentary.

"I think for you the routine is key," said Geoff. "You're like the King of Routine."

Whoa! Stop right there. King of Routine? I'm having that. Never mind an "effective entrepreneur," I'm the goddamn King of Routine!

So thank you, Geoff. Without that simple throwaway comment made after we'd stopped recording, I would never have fully embraced (or necessarily realised) just how important routine is to me – and this book would not exist. And so, dear reader, are you ready to find out how *you* can become a Routine Machine?

The King will see you now.

Homework

If you want new results, you need new routines. So here's your first new routine.

After every chapter, I'm going to ask you a few questions or set you tasks for you to complete. It's nothing too demanding; just a little something to get you thinking about what you've just read and how it applies to *your* life.

Now, I want you to *actually* stop and think about each question, even if it's only for 20 seconds. No moving on to the next chapter until you've done your homework!

Here's your first task.

Task: Over the next 24 hours, try to notice each decision you make. Was it the Human, the Monkey or the Computer that made that decision?

1. YOU ALREADY HAVE A ROUTINE

YOUR life is filled with routine. Successfully completing your homework from the last chapter will show you that, if you didn't know already. Look again and notice just how many tasks, jobs and decisions are automatically taken care of by the Computer.

You may even have a few ideas about how to tweak and improve those current routines, as well as introducing some new ones into the mix.

Don't fight this. I haven't written this book to tell you what routines you should implement in your life – I want you to find your own path, and to spark ideas for new (and improved) routines that work for *you* and *your* life. My job over the next few hundred pages is to give you that spark; to get you thinking about a number of things that you *could* change.

I'll let you know what's worked for me, as well as what hasn't. Towards the end of the book, I'll share a list of some of the routines that I've used, tweaked, improved and iterated over the last few years. It's a pretty long list, but yours doesn't have to be.

Maybe you want to change one big habit of a lifetime, 25 little ones or 300 micro-habits. Any of those paths will lead to a happier, less stressful life. Good routines help you grow and prosper. They ease the workload and make "doing the right thing" easy. You've got plenty of good routines already.

Bad routines can overwhelm you, and cause procrastination and frustration. They suck productive time out of your day and make "doing the wrong thing" easy. You've probably got more than a few bad routines in your arsenal too.

Go back over the last 24 hours and note how many of your current routines would fall into the "good" category and how many you'd class as "bad".

What's the split?

50/50? 60/40? 10/90?

It doesn't matter what the split is.

Correction.

It doesn't matter what the split is *right now*. What matters is what the split's going to be tomorrow. And next week. And next month. And next year.

If your split of good/bad routines is currently 10/90, then taking it to 15/85 is a decent result. That could be as simple as removing a single "hitting the snooze button" bad routine and implementing a solitary "read a bedtime story to my kids" good routine.

Your aim shouldn't be to completely eliminate all bad routines from your life. It should be to continually move the needle in the right direction and to aim for constant, never-ending improvement of the good/bad ratio.

Do you brush your teeth? Drive a car? Watch the same TV programmes at the same time every day or on the same night every week? Those are all routines. They're all things that you never used to do, but do now. And you do them on autopilot.

I like driving in my car

Do you remember when you first started learning to drive a car? How difficult was it to balance the clutch? Give it enough gas, but not too much. Now get the steering perfect. Look out for hazards in front of you. Oh, and check your mirrors. Yes, mirrors. Plural. There are three of them to check. Not to mention the hundreds of other cars zooming around you, all going in different directions and at different speeds.

But can you drive now?

If you can, then you probably don't think about any of that stuff anymore. You just get in the car and drive. More than likely, you can do all of those things while also listening to the radio, thinking about what you're going to have for tea that night and having a conversation with your passengers.

So why is it that what was once so hard is now easy and can be performed on autopilot?

When you first started, you had to learn each individual element of driving on its own. This is how to change from first gear to second gear. This is how to do a hill start. This is how you do a three-point-turn. And, slowly but surely, you started to put those elements together into a routine. Once you followed that same routine for a while, it became second nature. You don't need to consciously think about how to change from first to second gear anymore, it just happens. You're now thinking about how to parallel park instead, as you've mastered the basic routine.

And now, all these years later, what do you need to think about when you get in the car?

Nothing. You just drive.

You're still following the exact same routine that you were taught all those years ago. It's just that you've handed over the running of that routine – every single individual element from the hill starts to the gear changes – to your subconscious mind.

That's how it's possible to drive for miles on autopilot when your brain wanders without crashing and dying. If you've ever been driving and "zoned out" for part of the journey, that's your subconscious brain, the Computer, running your "driving a car" routine for you while you do something else.

Saturday night takeaway?

"Live from New York, it's Saturday Night!" There's no confusion over what night of the week Saturday Night Live is on the telly.

And what time's the News at Ten on?

When it comes to designing our routines, there are few people who know more about programming our brains to follow set patterns and routines on a regular basis than TV schedulers.

Even now, in the age of on-demand entertainment from Netflix and Amazon Prime, we're still hard-wired to watch television shows at the same time – whether that's the same time every day, the same day every week or to a well-established pattern (ask any soap addict and they'll able to tell you exactly when Corrie, EastEnders or Emmerdale are on).

Most shows fall into the "same time on the same day every week" category and this makes it really easy for you as a viewer to take the actions that the schedulers want you to – to keep watching. They want to make it as easy as possible for you to keep watching and they know that if they mess around with the schedule, you may accidentally miss an episode of something you'd otherwise continue to watch.

They also know that once you've missed one episode, you've broken the pattern of watching and are much less likely to seek out the show's new time slot and start watching again.

Say you like to watch Top Gear on a Sunday evening at 9pm on BBC Two. But midway through the series, they decide to move it to Wednesdays at 8pm. There are likely to be hundreds of thousands of people who tune in on Sunday evening at 9pm, only to find Dragons' Den or something else on instead.

The die-hard Top Gear fans will hunt down their favourite show's new time slot, but the more casual viewer will not. That's why rescheduling a TV show mid-series is a serious no-no, and for many a slot change has been the final nail in the coffin.

Doing the same thing at the same time on the same day every week is easy whether it's watching Doctor Who, doing football training, meeting a friend for coffee or going to the gym.

Don't lose your head

Your current routines may be conspiring against you. Every decision you make today affects your tomorrow. Everything compounds.

That burger you ate for lunch today doesn't really tip the scales, does it? Not on its own, no. But have a burger for lunch twice a week for a year and 10lbs of lard will "suddenly appear from nowhere" in the form of love handles and extra chins. All from one simple routine (what you ate for lunch).

You have hundreds of choices to make every day. Do you go to the pub with your mates or study for the test? Cook a healthy meal or order a pizza? Send out a sales letter or look at Facebook? Check your emails or play with your kids?

Every one of those decisions will either take you towards your goals or away from them.

Becoming a Routine Machine is about making good decisions automatically, taking away the willpower required to stay on the right path and without expending decision calories.

When a healthy lunch is "prepped" every day, you eat right. When Thursday nights are set aside for studying, you pass the test. When you close the laptop (and keep it shut!) before picking the kids up from school, you're always present. When you send a sales letter out every three months like clockwork, you keep the needle moving in the right direction.

Becoming a Routine Machine is as simple as creating routines that work for you and eliminating those that work against you.

Remember, I'm not here to tell you what routines you *should* implement in your life. That's entirely up to you, based on the goals you have and what you're looking to achieve. What I'll be aiming to do in this book is to give you some sparks of inspiration, and to share some things that have worked for me and some that have worked for others.

I'll show you examples of routines I had in place for years that were conspiring against me, actively sabotaging my hopes and dreams. Take it from me; achieving your goals when you're self-sabotaging is like trying to drive a car with the handbrake on.

I'll show you some of the tiny things that I've changed and I'll show you some of the massive, sweeping changes too. I'm still hacking away today, making little tweaks and large changes to my own Routine Machine with one aim – constant, never-ending improvement.

Every change I make to my routine does one of two things:

1. Improve the things that work for me – making me more likely to stick with the actions required to hit my goals.
2. Stop or reduce the actions that take me away from my goals. To eliminate self-sabotage.

Some of the most successful people in the world have gone "all-in" and become obsessed with these two distinctions. They ruthlessly cut out any action, any routine, and any time wasted on activities that take them away from their goals.

Real estate investor Grant Cardone talks about such actions as being "treasonous to your goals". Not just a waste of time or simply a bad idea, but "treasonous". That's a word that brings to mind a vivid picture of people literally losing their heads.

When you treat routines that conspire against you as seriously as you would a betrayal against the King or Queen punishable by death, it's much harder to make excuses for such behaviour.

Reframing the behaviour you'd like to change and portraying it as infinitely more negative is a very effective way to instigate change and makes it much, much easier to say "no" without using any willpower. And Cardone does this with the idea that such actions are "treasonous to his goals".

Former Navy SEAL Jocko Willink reframes sugar as poison. "Those doughnuts aren't food. They are poison. Same with that chocolate chip cookie – poison. The double-Dutch chocolate cake? Poison. The can of soda, the bag of potato chips and the pretzel-wrapped hot dog? All poison. That junk isn't food. It doesn't fuel you. It kills you. Literally kills you."

I did the same when I gave up drinking alcohol back in 2013. I reframed the booze from a nice drink that I used to relax, unwind and socialise into a drug. And I don't take drugs. Alcohol was now reframed in my mind and filed away in my Computer alongside heroin, crack cocaine and crystal meth as just one more drug that I don't take.

I've never relaxed by sniffing glue on a Friday night and I've never fancied having a few rounds of meth with my buddies at the football. No one has ever asked me if I fancied "a quick half of heroin for the road", and I don't recall adverts proclaiming to offer "probably the best crack cocaine in the world".

The minute I reframed alcohol in my mind as "just another drug I don't take", saying no to it became easy. I could walk down the beer and wine aisle in Sainsbury's and not be tempted in the slightest, because in my mind I might as well have been walking down the marijuana and ecstasy aisle.

The real beauty of hacking your routines, adding and improving those that work for you and reducing or removing those that work against you, is the fact that it all compounds over time. Eat that burger twice a week and go up a trouser size. Go to the gym twice a week and drop a trouser size.

Drop the twice-weekly burger *and* go to the gym and you'll drop *two* trouser sizes.

Compounding works both ways. Stack up negative routines and they'll compound to work against you. Treason! Stack up positive ones and they'll compound to propel you towards your goals.

Why not trade off a negative routine in fair exchange for a positive one? Find something negative you're currently devoting too much time to and allocate that time instead to something more positive.

Don't be a traitor to your goals. You might just lose your head.

Consistently not stupid

I'm a big fanboy of Warren Buffett, the billionaire investor behind Berkshire Hathaway and one of the world's richest men.

But that's not why I love the "Oracle of Omaha". Sure, his net worth is estimated at $86billion at the time of writing (it was *only* $67billion when I wrote my previous book in 2017, so it's fair to say he's had a decent few years), but that's just a number.

What I love about Buffett (and his business partner Charlie Munger) is the fact that he's the most down-to-earth, genuine billionaire I know.

Eighty-six billion dollars hasn't changed the man one inch. He lives in the same house he bought for $31,500 in 1958. He buys cheap cars and drives them for decades. He never spends more than $3.17 on breakfast (he'll only spend $2.95 if the market was flat the day before and go even cheaper at $2.61 if the Dow Jones drops).

He earns caviar and champagne money, but is strictly a cheeseburger and Coke guy.

But don't dismiss him as a penny-pinching hoarder. You don't end up as one of the richest guys on the planet, amassing almost a hundred billion dollars, simply by cutting coupons and turning down your heating.

Buffett and Munger have made serious money over a sustained period of time. They've lived through countless recessions, seen thousands and thousands of companies vanish from existence and yet continue to grow at a consistent rate of almost 20 per cent per year. And they've done it for decades.

They dodged the tech crash of 2000 and the global financial crisis of 2008.

How the hell have they delivered returns that consistent in an inconsistent marketplace? By being consistent. Or as Munger puts it: "Consistently not stupid".

While everyone else is trying to be clever, Buffett and Munger are trying to "avoid being stupid". They don't try to time the market. They don't try to guess which stock is going up and which is going down. They didn't get burned by the tech crash in 2000, because they didn't ride the wave of the tech boom in the late 90s.

They weren't brought down by the global financial crisis in 2008, because they didn't stick their paws in the honeypots of sub-prime mortgage lending or trading derivatives.

They stuck with what they know.

Munger likens this approach to tennis. Amateur players try to return every shot, trying to out-trick their opponent and guess what they're going to do next. They try audacious shots that have a low chance of success. They often lose more points due to their own attempts at winning than they would if they simply focused on getting the shot returned back over the net.

That's not how professionals play – either in tennis, in football, in golf, in the stock market or in business. Professionals play for points. They focus on not losing first and cutting out the silly mistakes – the haphazard attempt to score a wonder goal rather than passing to your team-mate for a tap-in.

Let me repeat this point: They focus on *not losing* first.

Keep on not losing and eventually your opponent will make a mistake, *they'll* do something stupid and *you'll* win. Professionals cut out stupid first.

Buffett's first rule of investing?

"Never lose money."

And rule number two?

"Never forget rule number one."

The easiest way to win is to never lose, and the easiest way to never lose is to be consistently not stupid.

Doctor Who doing a stock check

Because so much of our lives are run on autopilot, with our Computer in charge of things, it's often difficult to know what routines we're actually following on a daily basis. If you've ever uttered the words, "I don't know where the day went" then you'll know what I'm talking about.

So, how do we find out where the day went? Or the week? Or the month? Or the year? We do a time audit.

This may sound like Doctor Who doing a stock check, but it's actually a really useful exercise that I found very revealing when I first did it.

Creating your first-time audit is a piece of cake. Simply set a reminder or alarm on your phone to go off every 15 minutes. Every time it goes off, write down in a few words what you've spent the last 15 minutes doing.

Don't worry if you've been doing lots of different things in that last quarter of an hour, just note down the one thing that you spent most of that time doing. You can use a spreadsheet or good old fashioned pen and paper. Don't obsess over the tech.

It'll start to look something like this:

09:00 Email
09:10 Email
09:30 Facebook
09:45 Phone call (customer)
10:00 Admin
10:15 Facebook
10:30 Meeting (staff)
10:45 Meeting (staff)
11:00 Coffee break
11:15 Daydreaming

Fill it in for an entire working day and do it for a whole week, by the end of which you should have 160 entries (assuming a 40-hour working week). Once you have a week's worth, it's time to analyse the data and start creating some five-bar gates as we tally up each task.

You should now have a list of things that you can put in order from the most time spent to the least and see exactly how you actually spend your working week. You may think (or be able to convince yourself) that you've been pretty productive working on your big sales campaign all week long, but when the audit reveals that you actually only spent five hours on it compared to six hours "browsing Facebook", there's nowhere to hide.

Your final list could look something like this:

Writing copy	5.25 hours
Emails and admin	5 hours
Meetings	4.5 hours
Facebook (productive)	4.25 hours
Coaching	4 hours
Facebook (unproductive)	3.75 hours
Speaking with staff	2.75 hours
Procrastinating	2.25 hours
Don't know!	2 hours
Dealing with interruptions	0.75 hours

That's the top ten from one of my most recent audits during a week that I thought I'd spent the whole time writing copy and coaching clients. Yet the audit showed I actually only spent around a quarter of my time doing that.

It showed me I was wasting almost as much time dicking around on Facebook as I was doing productive work on there. It showed me I lose almost an hour a week to interruptions. That's a whole working week over the course of a year!

I found out I spent far too long dealing with emails and admin and that our meetings went on too long. I also lost a good couple of hours by procrastinating. But most worrying of all was the two hours lost time to "Don't know".

An alarm went off to remind me to write down, in that exact moment, what I had just spent the last 15 minutes doing. Even though I was sat at my desk "working", I honestly couldn't answer what the hell I had actually been doing for the last quarter of an hour!

This is where your time goes: Day-dreaming, procrastination, interruptions, meetings and admin.

Once you've got the results of your time audit, it's time to decide what needs to change. If you want different results, you need different routines.

After seeing my audit results, I installed a Facebook news feed blocker on my computer so I could still access the productive side of social media, but not get distracted by videos of cream egg cheesecakes. I employed a part-time admin. I asked my business partner Jason Brockman to act as chairman in all our meetings to keep us on a strict agenda and to massively reduce the time spent in meetings. I also now turn my phone to Do Not Disturb and never answer the door when I'm doing deep work.

How many legs does a dog have if you call the tail a leg?

Four.

Calling a tail a leg doesn't make it a leg. *Saying* you spent all day doing productive work doesn't mean you *actually* did spend all day doing productive work.

Stop lying to yourself over how you *actually* spend your days. Do a time audit and find out the truth.

A chicken walks into a library

A chicken walks into a library and says, "Bock."

Confused, but intrigued, the librarian hands him a book. The chicken takes it and goes merrily on his way.

The next day, the chicken is back. He struts up to the counter and says, "Bock, bock." The librarian hands him two books.

This happens again on day three – "Bock, bock, bock" – and the librarian hands over three books.

On the fifth day, the librarian's curiosity gets the better of her and she follows the chicken to see what he's actually doing with all these books.

Then she sees a frog sitting in a quiet corner of the library.

The chicken approaches the frog, places the five books into the frog's hands and says, "Bock, bock, bock, bock, bock."

The frog responds by tossing each book aside one by one.

"Reddit."

"Reddit."

"Reddit."

"Reddit."

"Reddit."

I've met so many people like that frog. They're prolific readers, often getting through at least a book a week. That's a pretty healthy routine to have, right?

Well, it depends what you *do* with all that new knowledge and insight. If all you do after reading a book is toss it aside, say "reddit" and move onto the next one, then you're missing a crucial piece of the jigsaw.

Reading books doesn't make you healthy, wealthy or wise. Reading books and then *implementing* what you've just learned does.

Samwell Tarly discovered this in season seven of the epic drama Game of Thrones when he cured Jorah Mormont of the "incurable" greyscale disease by poring through dozens and dozens of ancient textbooks.

When asked by the Elders how he achieved such an inconceivable, impossible feat, Sam replies rather modestly: "Well... I read the books... and followed the instructions..."

The knowledge sat on those shelves gathering dust for hundreds of years. Wise men, elder statesmen and – dare I say it – "experts" had *read* the books. But having read the books, they then tossed the information aside like the frog in the library.

"Reddit."

They didn't change a thing as a result of reading it.

Read the book and follow the instructions. It really is that easy.

I recently added a new routine to ensure that I follow this rule. Every time I finish reading a non-fiction book, I don't allow myself to start another until I've written a "book report" on what I've just read. This can take any format from an 800-word blog post, a five-minute Facebook Live to our One Percenters or a quick email to my subscribers listing my key takeaways from the book.

Crucially, I'll also decide on at least one thing that I'm actually going to *do* as a result of reading those few hundred pages.

If nothing changes, you've wasted your time reading the book.

Don't just "read the book" – read the book and follow the instructions.

568ml of fizzy water

Can a book brainwash you in less than three chapters? That's what happened to me back in 2013. I got very drunk one Saturday night and decided that I'd like to cut back on the sauce a little. Maybe just partake once or twice a month. Just become a social drinker.

That night, I made my best ever drunken purchase. I went online, ordered a copy of *'Kick The Drink...Easily'* by Jason Vale and stumbled off to bed.

The following day, as I lay dying on the sofa with the mother of all hangovers, I whipped out my Kindle (other reading devices are available) and started reading. By the time I'd finished the third chapter, I'd changed my mind. I no longer wanted to just cut back on my drinking – I didn't want to drink ever again.

What caused that change in thinking? Words. Written on a page.

Sure, I had to be in the right place to *want* to quit drinking. But what Jason Vale did in those first few chapters was to change who I am and how I think about myself. When I opened the book and started reading Chapter One, I was a hungover bloke who wanted some "hacks" to help him cut down on the booze.

By Chapter Four, I was a non-drinker.

Of course, it wasn't quite that simple. By Chapter Four, I'd made the *decision* to become a non-drinker. I'd read the book, but I still needed to follow the instructions.

Unfortunately, mere words don't turn a drunk into a teetotaller. You have to actually do the work too. And it was hard work.

The "resisting drink" urge wasn't hard. I was pretty clear that I didn't want to drink, full-stop. But I needed to change loads of my existing routines to account for my new-found sobriety.

Friday afternoon at the pub. A few beers at the footy. A bottle of wine and a takeaway on a Saturday night. Work nights out. Attending a conference; "Meet you at the bar?"

It would be very easy for me to become like the character Nana from the Royle Family, who "doesn't drink at all…except for a bottle of stout of an evening and a sherry at Christmas…and Champagne at weddings…and a whisky at New Year".

The hardest part about giving up alcohol wasn't going without the booze itself, it was dealing with other people's reactions and expectations around my decision.

I'll never forget when I told my business partner Jason. We were at an entrepreneurs' conference in Basingstoke (see kids, this is the rock and roll lifestyle I lead) and as per our usual routine, we drove up the day before and headed to the bar.

"I'll get these in," I said, and a few minutes later I returned to our table with a pint of lager and a pint of sparkling water. I was met with the blankest face I've ever seen. It's not often that Jason is lost for words, but he was totally gobsmacked by this sudden revelation. And it's easy to see why. Jason and I were "pint of lager" drinkers, not sissy sparkling water. As Al Murray, the Pub Landlord tells us, it's "a pint for the fella, glass of white wine/fruit-based drink for the lady".

Predictable.

So when I returned to the table with 568ml of fizzy water, alarm bells started going off in Jason's head.

"What's up with you?" he asked.

"Oh. Er. I don't feel like drinking at the moment."

That was the line I used for the first two months: "I don't feel like drinking at the moment."

But it wasn't true. I was lying to everyone. I used that "don't feel like it right now" line as a backup in case I failed and fell off the wagon. After all, I gave up at the start of November and still had the peak drinking season of Christmas and New Year to get through. And get through it I did.

Who knew that by not staying up drinking Jack Daniels till 2am on Christmas Eve, I'd wake up hangover-free on Christmas Day for the first time in 15 years? Or that I'd actually remember *everything* that happened on New Year's Eve (and not have to wait three hours for a taxi)?

As soon as I'd made it past New Year's Eve, I knew I could start telling people the truth: "I don't drink."

It's easier to say that now; it flows off the tongue. It's *who I am* now. I'm a non-drinker.

I gave up smoking in 2006 and for the first few months I was a smoker who was trying to quit. That was who I was. And then suddenly, *who I was* changed. I became a non-smoker.

If you want to change who you are, you need to change your routines.

I now happily tell people that I don't drink, answer their questions (One: No, I don't miss it. Two: Yes, I do feel so much better for it. Three: No, it wasn't really that hard), and I can tell them exactly how I did it.

I read the book and I followed the instructions.

Homework

Question 1: What percentages of your current routines are working for you?

Question 2: What percentages of your current routines are working against you?

Question 3: What can you tell me about the last book you read (before this one)?

2. BUILDING MY ROUTINE MACHINE

Who ate all the pies?

You know all those weight loss programmes, diet books, exercise videos, "meal in a bottle" fads and the like? They all use the same technique to sell the benefits and to convince your sceptical brain that their system or plan works where others have failed for you.

Ladies and gentlemen of the jury, I present to you exhibit A: The before picture.

This is *my* "before" picture. It was taken in a bar in Spain in 2003 when I was 25 years old. And what a picture of health I look – cigarette hanging out of my mouth, glazed slightly-drunken expression and looking like I've been inflated with a ton of air.

I was around five stone overweight at this point and this is the most unflattering photo of me that I have from that time. It's the perfect "before" picture.

Except it's not. You see, there was a "before" before this.

A "before" when I wasn't fat. A "before" when I didn't smoke. A "before" when I didn't drink. A "before" when I actually got some exercise beyond walking from the pub to the kebab shop.

I didn't suddenly wake up one day and find that I'd gained 70lbs or that someone had sneaked into my wardrobe overnight and replaced all my clothes with ones that are three or four sizes too small for me.

I didn't take up smoking just for the purposes of this picture. Nor did I decide to neck eight pints of lager just for the effect it would have on my complexion.

You see, this "before" photo is actually the "after" photo. It was taken after several years of small habits and routines, including:

- Smoking just one cigarette...per hour...every day.
- Eating one greasy takeaway...two to three times a week.
- Getting between five and six hours' sleep most nights and pulling one all-nighter each week.
- Drinking one pint of lager. Then another. Repeat times 30. Every weekend.
- Eating a nice, easy, processed ready-meal...twice a day.
- Grabbing cereal as an easy snack...daily.
- Sitting at my desk without moving (except for cigarette breaks) for 16 hours per day.

From 1997 to 2003, that was my routine. That's what I did, day in, day out, week after week, month after month. It's no mystery that I ended up looking like the Michelin Man after compounding that routine for six years.

There was a "before" before the before picture. There's always a before. Where you are *right now* is the compound effect of every decision you've ever made and all of your habits and routines thus far. Compare any two photos of yourself taken at different times in your life and think about what caused the changes (good or bad) between the two.

The answer is everything you did routinely between those two dates. The food you ate. The drugs you took. The friends you kept. The work you did. The sleep you got. The exercise you did. The people you loved. The fun you had. The way you beat yourself up. The number of birthday candles you blew out.

If you want your current photo to become your "before" picture then you need to change what you do consistently.

Of course, you could go to the gym five times a week and go on a crash diet for a month and you'd probably lose a ton of weight. But you won't keep that up, and if you go back to the old routine then you'll go back to the old results.

If you want new results, you need new routines.

It took me several years to gain those 70lbs and it took me several years to lose them too. But lose them I did and they've stayed away for the last seven years now.

So what routines did I change?

The first thing I did was to cut out processed food from my evening meal. One change. I saw some results.

So I added going to the gym once a week. More results came. I added "no takeaways on weekdays" as a rule. Then I gave up smoking. The gym got easier as a result of not smoking, so I went twice a week. More results.

I gave up the booze. Then I gave up fizzy, sugary drinks. Then I started juicing fruit and vegetables.

That was everything I needed to do to drop all the excess weight and look and feel better than I had in a decade. But it didn't happen overnight. Everything I've just said happened over a five-year period.

If I'd tried to put all of those routines in place on day one and gone from being a chain-smoking, beer-swilling slob to a gym freak who drinks pints of broccoli and celery every day, it's fair to say those routines wouldn't have lasted long and I'd have soon lapsed back into my old routine.

What worked for me was changing *one* routine. Seeing some results from that one change then made me want to make another. And as that change compounded and brought even more positive feedback, I was driven to improve every aspect of my health routine.

Even now, years after losing all that weight, I'm still experimenting with different ways to improve my health routine with intermittent fasting, improved sleep, better mitochondrial function, HIIT training and cold therapy on the list of things I'm currently testing and tweaking.

How I 10x'ed my business, using one sheet of A4

Back in 2012, I was juggling ten to 12 small businesses and I was doing everything for all of them. I was chief content writer, customer service agent, admin person and tea boy.

I'd spend some time writing content for our mobile phone insurance website. Then write a press release for our serviced offices business, before collating photos for our travel website. A quick break to answer emails from customers about sex toys, breakdown cover and live football streaming, and then I could settle down to start the advertising copy for our bingo brand.

The next day would be completely different. If I were to describe my strategy in one word, it would be "random".

When it came to planning out my days – how I was going to effectively run up to 12 businesses and ultimately provide me and my team with our livelihood – I was leaving it all to chance.

I had no routine whatsoever. I simply reacted to whatever landed on my desk next and whoever shouted the loudest.

The problem was that it had worked, up to a point. Each of those businesses was making a bit of money and I was doing OK. Sure, I was working harder than I needed and none of those businesses ever had my full attention, but what was it costing me?

It didn't take long for me to find out. Later that year, Google gave me a good hard kick in the balls in the form of their now famous "Panda" and "Penguin" updates, which they rolled out in the space of a single year.

These updates targeted two known problems that were affecting the quality of Google's search engine results – low-quality on-page content and low-quality inbound links.

And guess what?

Yep, our businesses had shedloads of both. Literally overnight, we went from receiving an average of 100,000 visitors a month from Google to less than 1,000. Google just turned off the tap, overnight.

What I was now left with was a load of almost worthless businesses. And one that kept us in the game.

I had one business that wasn't entirely reliant on Google traffic. It had its own mailing list, Twitter following and Facebook page. It had loyal customers who returned to the website every day, and who looked out for our emails arriving in their inbox on a daily basis.

We were part of those customers' daily routine.

I knew that I needed to focus on this particular business and I knew that I needed to do a lot more marketing. Not just one-off, big marketing campaigns when we had a sale or some massive promotion that we were pushing, but to be routinely marketing to our members day in and day out.

If you want new results, you need new routines.

I created a document that, to this day, is the single best piece of marketing I've ever created. And it was so simple.

It was one sheet of A4, and I called it my "daily marketing planner". The business was a sports betting service, which offered football tips, horse racing tips and statistical analysis. Every day, these services would send out tips to their members.

I had some blank space on the daily marketing planner to write in those tips, which I would do first thing in the morning. Then I'd go about my day doing customer support, tweaking sales pages on the website, writing social media copy, etc.

At the end of the day (after all the horses had run and all the football matches were over), I'd get out my daily marketing planner again and see how the tips had got on.

What followed next was a simple flow chart. Did we have a big-priced winner on our email list? Post on Facebook to ensure people have joined the mailing list. Did our Premium Tip win for the third time in a row? Send out an email with a link to the service sign-up page. Are we one game away from landing a 22/1 accumulator on the football? Post on Twitter to let members know.

The daily marketing planner documented everything that we *could* do on a daily basis to market the products to our members. Most times, we'd ignore 80 per cent of the options. But by following a *daily* marketing planner, we were building a new daily routine (marketing our business) that we knew would pay dividends in the long run as long as we kept doing it every day.

And so it proved.

That single sheet of A4 forced us to create the routine of daily marketing and quadrupled the size of the business over the next 18 months. The turnover doubled again in the following 18 months and now, as our sports betting business celebrates its

11th birthday, the business is ten times the size it was before I printed off that first sheet of A4.

That business now employs five full-time members of staff and they still use the daily marketing planner to this day.

Just survive the next three weeks

My world was turned upside down at Christmas 2008, with four little words: "I think I'm pregnant."

Fast forward to August 2009 (I swear it *did* go that quickly too!), and Jack Robert Lamerton, son and heir to the Lamerton empire, was born. It was an empire that, at the time, consisted of a bingo website, some Lloyds TSB shares and a handful of Premium Bonds.

Sarah and I were new to this parenting lark. We'd done some uncle-ing and auntie-ing before, but no actual parenting. Much to our shock and horror, the nurses at the hospital didn't seem too concerned about this as they let us leave the hospital, baby in tow, without so much as a pamphlet, let alone an instruction manual.

I had more information about how to care for my dishwasher than I did how to look after this miniature human, who by the looks of him didn't have a self-cleaning function or a quiet mode!

We somehow get him home, driving at 15 miles per hour the whole way, and pop him in his nice new Moses basket. He seems happy enough for now, but when do we feed him? What if he gets ill? What if something happens and we don't know what to do? He looks really small and delicate. Are we going to break him? And most importantly, when are *we* going to sleep now?

All valid questions, I'm sure you'll agree. So I went to the only place I know to get answers that I trust.

The internet.

Specifically, friends of mine on the internet.

Even more specifically, friends of mine on the internet who already had kids.

We received all manner of advice about breastfeeding, nappy changes, colic, weaning, potty training, and which school to get him on the waiting list for.

But we weren't ready for that. Our main concern was what to do right here, right now. Sleepless nights. Screaming baby. *That* was what we were worried about.

My mate Chris sent me the following advice, which I've subsequently shared with any new parents I've spoken with:

> *"Get baby into a routine ASAP. Feed at the same times, a bath at the same time, bed at the same time. Every day. Start now. It'll take about three weeks. Just survive the next three weeks and then it'll get easier."*

So that's what we did. We planned the feeds around when Jack seemed to want feeding. We changed his nappy on demand and started a "bath then bed" routine on a daily basis at the same time every night.

As Chris had warned, the next three weeks were indeed really tough. There was no set routine to when Jack would wake and demand feeding, changing or just fancied having a look at Mummy and Daddy at 4.30 in the morning.

Eventually, though, things settled down and Jack fell in with our routine, which of course we'd sculpted around his natural "empty belly/full nappy" demands, but which was also devised with the concept that Mummy and Daddy might actually get some sleep too.

Sarah and I would "work" different shifts at night. I was a night-owl pre-children, so I was happy to sit up watching Chuck Norris movies and every episode of Road Wars ever made on a nightly basis until Jack woke for his 1am feed, which I would deliver and then head to bed myself.

This allowed Sarah to hit the sack around 9pm and clock up a good seven or eight hours of *fairly* uninterrupted sleep (you're never going to sleep like a log with your firstborn baby in the room) before Master Lamerton would try to get us to join the 5am club by demanding his next feed.

Spoiler alert. We survived the first three weeks.

And it was all thanks to getting that simple feed, bath and then bed routine in place. It's a routine that remains in place ten years later – even if there is now a two-hour delay between the bath and Jack actually going to sleep.

Second spoiler alert. The dishwasher broke.

Sir Chew-a-lot

We recently had another bundle of joy enter the Lamerton household. Chewie is a two-month-old cockapoo puppy. Yes, he's named after Chewbacca from the Star Wars movies. He's just as hairy, but not quite as tall and he hasn't got the opposable thumbs to operate a bowcaster.

The name suits him down to the ground, though, as he likes nothing better than chewing on my slippers or my laptop bag or my shoelaces. Or my hand.

It's been seven years since we had a baby (Jack's brother, Harry) in the house, but within a few hours of Chewie's arrival it was time to dust off the "just survive the first three weeks" routine. The breeder left us with a set of "rules". I don't know if they included "don't get him wet" and "don't feed him after midnight", but it felt like we were taking home a mogwai for the first time.

Rule number one, she warned us, was that we were the leaders of the pack. Top Dogs. If there's a pecking order, Chewie's at the bottom of it. Sarah and I are at the top, then the kids, then Jinx (our Springer), Ruby the cat, and finally Sir Chew-a-lot.

He is to fit in with *our* routine, not the other way around.

Got it. What's next?

Food: Jinx gets one decent scoopful of kibble in the morning. Chewie, by comparison, needs feeding five times a day at 7am, 11am, 3pm, 7pm and 11pm. We need to count out the number of pieces of kibble he gets. Seventeen is the magic number.

Toilet training: He's made some progress on this already and keeps his pen clean, emptying his bladder on newspaper. We now need to train him that the best place to do all of his *business* is outside in the garden. This means I get to carry him outside once every hour in all weathers. And Chewie doesn't like rain. So if it's damp at all, I know full well what's going to happen.

I'll carry him from the kitchen to the garden (which requires going up three steps, along a balcony, down ten steps, across the patio, and down another four steps), stand him on the grass and utter the immortal words which would fill any man with masculine pride: "Come on Chewie, time for a wee-wee."

Before I've even got the word "wee-wee" out, Chewie's decided "bugger this for a game of soldiers" and has started sprinting back inside. He's already across the patio and halfway up the large set of steps before I've reached the first one. I traipse up the rest of the steps, pick him up and take him back down to the grass to repeat the process.

At least I'm getting my 10,000 steps in.

We do this three or four times (depending on how hard it's raining) and I'm usually the one who gives in, eventually relenting and coming back into the nice dry house where, ten minutes later, Chewie will decide he really *does* need a wee-wee after all and does so on the living room floor.

According to the instruction manual that came with Chewie, he usually wakes at 3am. "You might want to refresh his hot water bottle at this point," says the manual. I don't think so.

We had enough sleepless nights with the two children, so there's no chance I'm getting up at 3am to refresh his hot water bottle, plump his pillows or place a mint on his bedcovers.

I think back to when Jinx was a pup. The first night, she howled the house down. We went into her 20 times. We fed her, played with her and cuddled her. And she was perfectly happy while we were in the room, but would whine like mad the minute we left. The following morning, she'd be bright as a daisy and we felt like death.

Night two, and she started howling again. This time we ignored her. We sneaked up to the kitchen door to check she was OK, but without her seeing us. She was fine. We went back to bed.

Three hours she whined. We got some sleep, but not much.

Night three, and she slept through. As did we. Victory was ours.

So no, I was not going to be visiting Chewie at three in the morning. Sure enough, on the first night he woke around three. He whined for about 20 minutes and we didn't hear from him again until the morning.

Night two, he woke at 4am and cried for a few minutes. Again, we ignored him and he settled again.

Night three, we didn't hear a peep out of him.

Finally, he's fitting in with *our* routine, rather than us fitting into his. Now if I could just get him to stop eating my slippers.

The world's largest snowball

In my mind, compounding is the closest thing you can get to a secret weapon – certainly when it comes to investing, growing businesses and building long-lasting wealth.

I was first introduced to the concept in Robert Kiyosaki's *'Rich Dad Poor Dad'* and my learning on it was compounded (pun very much intended) by the Oracle of Omaha, Warren Buffett. As is often the way, Buffett is able to sum up complex things in simple ways.

All you need to be able to understand and take advantage of the power of compounding is this one sentence from Buffett:

> *"Life is like a snowball; all you need is wet snow and a really long hill."*

This is how Buffett and his partner in crime Charlie Munger have achieved an average 20.9 per cent annual return for more than five decades.

They didn't have much snow to begin with, but they've had a hell of a long hill to roll it down and their snowball could literally move mountains now. If you'd invested £10,000 with Buffett and Munger back in 1965, you'd have been sat on £270million by the end of 2018. And by the time you read this book, it would have more than likely "snowballed" further to more than £300million!

Berkshire Hathaway (Buffett and Munger's holding company) doesn't pay dividends to its shareholders and it never has. Rather than paying out profits to shareholders every year, it re-invests every single penny into buying bigger stakes in great companies like Coca-Cola, American Express and Gillette.

It compounds all their returns into more stock. More assets. More snow.

Buffett and Munger don't have "side-hustles" either. Everything they do and everything they own is in Berkshire Hathaway. And over nearly six decades, they've methodically and deliberately designed and built the world's largest snowball – owning 26 per cent of Heinz, 17 per cent of American Express, nine per cent of Coca-Cola, seven per cent of the Bank of America and five per cent of Apple.

Oh, and they've also got more than $100,000,000,000 in cash.

One hundred BILLION dollars in surplus cash.

That's one hell of a snowball.

My little snowflakes

I did a talk recently with the amazingly click-baity title of "How I made 8,000+% ROI from Lifestyle Businesses".

While I'm not a fan of the spammy title, the concept is true. I really have achieved those sorts of returns from running lifestyle businesses. But we're not talking about passive investments here. You can't just take your money out of the Post Office, cash in your Premium Bonds and pop it in an 8,000 per cent tracker ISA.

The only way I can achieve those sorts of gains is through compounding (or snowballing), especially in the very early years.

When I started my first business back in 2000, I compounded every single penny it made – mainly because it wasn't making very many pennies and there was no other way I could afford to actually grow the business.

But, as it started making a little bit of money, I resisted the temptation to take a few quid out and instead continued to snowball it – packing every single flake of snow back on and rolling it down the hill.

Even when I started earning enough to give up a day job I hated, I stuck it out for several months longer, going part-time first to keep as many of those tiny, wet snowflakes on my newly-formed snowball as possible rather than spending them on living expenses.

And that habit has stuck with me in business after business that I've launched. In almost every new venture I've gone into over the last 20 years, I always aim to "snowball" (re-invest) all profits for at least 18 months.

My very first business, Net Free Stuff, was started with a £100 overdraft. I snowballed everything into learning more about how business works, learning all about marketing, better design, software, etc. I owned that business for five years, before selling it for £120,000.

How did I turn £100 into £120,000? I snowballed it.

When I could afford it, I upgraded the website from free hosting to paid. Then I moved from a shared server to a dedicated server. Later, I got an actual designer to make me a logo after "knocking one up" myself. Then I bought some email marketing software, started some paid advertising and eventually took on my first member of staff. Then my second. I then paid to go to conferences and seminars and continued learning.

Even when I finally gave up the day job from hell, I still paid myself quite a bit less than the business was actually earning. In the beginning, I did that as a safety net in case "this internet thing" didn't work out and I had to find another "real" job. I figured living below my means and saving the rest would buy me a few months to pay the bills while I worked on my CV.

Soon though, it became apparent that not only was "this internet thing" not going away, it actually presented me with several opportunities to grow and all I had to do was keep rolling that snowball down the hill.

Some years later, I bought a live football streaming business for £6,250. In this business, I focused our initial snowball-building efforts into improving the conversion rate on the website. I attended a two-day conference in London and watched presentations by experts in conversion rate optimisation to see how the big boys like Amazon and the BBC do it.

I approached the speakers after their talk and enquired about working with them. "We charge £5,000 per month with a minimum six-month term," were almost the first words out of their mouths. If their intention was to scare me away with large prices, job done! I'd just invested the grand sum of £6,250 in buying the business, so finding a further £30,000 at that stage simply wasn't an option.

So, instead, I copied what they showed me in their talks and did the conversion rate optimisation work myself. I "read the book and followed the instructions".

As a result of this work, every single visitor to the website was now worth more money. Instead of 0.3 per cent of visitors buying, I was now persuading 2.2 per cent of them to part with some cash. I'd just increased my profitability seven-fold!

Because we were now earning seven times more money per visitor to the website, it opened up Google AdWords as a marketing channel that had been previously cost-prohibitive. We could now afford to advertise profitably in a place where we'd have previously lost our shirts.

We snowballed just about everything we had into Google ads and continued improvements in conversion rate optimisation. The more money each website visitor was worth, the more advertising we could afford. And the more advertising we did, the more website visitors we got.

More visitors worth more money paying to get more visitors who are worth more money.

You can see how this soon snowballs. We earned around half a million pounds in this business over a three-year period, before the legislation around live streaming changed and we decided to shut the service down.

Half a million quid from a six-grand investment. That's one of my favourite snowballs.

The £25million snowball

I'm no longer snowballing businesses for 18 months. I'm now building a truly massive snowball instead and rolling it down a 20-plus-year hill.

I started my first business in 2000 with a £100 overdraft. Over the last two decades, I've snowballed that £100 into a pretty big empire, owning several businesses, a load of property and several investments that now throw off excess cash every year.

I say this not to impress you with where I am now, but to impress *upon* you where I was 20 years ago.

I had £100 of someone else's money. I knew nothing. I didn't know how to run a business. I didn't know how to get and keep customers. I knew nothing of pricing or evaluating investments. I had no assets. No knowledge. No expertise. No resources. No experience. No clue.

Twenty years later though, and it's a very different picture. I've got money behind me now. I've got a network full of millionaires. I've got years and years of experience and continue to study to close my knowledge gap.

Buffett and Munger have racked up $100billion in cash and own huge chunks of Coke, Amex and Gillette.

Jason and I haven't done anywhere near as well as Warren and Charlie, but we are following in their footsteps, albeit on a much, much smaller scale.

We've accumulated a decent six-figure pile of excess cash and own a nice chunk of a sports betting company, a mortgage brokerage, a business coaching platform, an online tutoring business, and some other investments that all throw off excess cash every year.

We're in the rather nice position of having more money than we need. It's the same position I was in back in 2002 when Net Free Stuff earned £1,500 a month and I only needed £1,100 to pay the bills – but on a slightly bigger scale.

Just as I did back in 2002 with a £400 a month surplus, rather than waste excess cash by buying useless junk I neither need nor want, I'm packing that snow right back onto my snowball and I'm rolling it down the next two-decade hill.

Here's my thinking:

I'm starting with £100,000 cash. I'm then going to add £100,000 every single year. I'm aiming to grow my snowball by 20 per cent compounded annual growth (the same as Buffett and Munger have achieved by being "consistently not stupid" for the last five decades) for at least the next 20 years.

If I achieve this, in three years I should have £575,000. After five years, that's doubled to £1million-plus. Twelve years in and it becomes £5million. Four more years and it doubles again to £10million. And finally, after 20 years, my snowball would be worth more than £25,000,000.

I'll have put £2.1million into the pot and compounding will have grown it to £25million in 20 years. That sounds unbelievable, doesn't it?

But where did that first £2.1million come from?

It came from a £100 overdraft and a bloke who knew nothing 20 years ago. If I can turn £100 into £2.1million in 20 years, there's no reason I can't turn £2.1million into £25million in another 20. I just need to keep packing on that snow.

But it's not snowing yet!

You don't need £100,000 a year in excess cash to start packing on the snow. You just need a few tiny flakes. As I said, my entire journey started with a £100 overdraft.

Don't fall into the trap of waiting until you've got something worth compounding – start now. The finite resource isn't the money or the success or fame, it's the time. And the longer you wait, the shorter your hill is going to be.

But the longer the hill, the fewer snowflakes you need to add in the first place.

At 20 per cent annual growth (compounded), you need a lump sum of £163,000 to have a cool million after ten years. To achieve the same in 20 years, you only need to start with £26,500. And if you've got a nice 40-year hill in front of you, then £681 will get you there.

Yep, roll a £681 snowball down a 40-year hill and you'll find a million-pound snowball at the bottom.

Add £20 a month to it as well, and it nearly trebles in size!

As I write this, Warren Buffett is 88 years old and Charlie Munger recently celebrated his 95th birthday. When asked to name the top three things that made him the world's most successful investor, Buffett replied: "Living in America for the great opportunities, having good genes so I lived a long time, and compound interest."

Taking opportunities, compounding your gains and having a nice long hill of time. That's it. That's the "secret" to Buffett's success.

Whether you've got a cool million in the bank already, a spare hundred grand to invest every year or access to a £100 overdraft and a copy of *'Internet Marketing for Dummies'*, you can start to collect whatever snowflakes are falling around you and start crafting your snowball.

Are we there yet?

I earned £13.51 from my first nine months in business. Nine months later, I quit my day job. And nine months after that, I was earning more than £100k a year.

Warren Buffett bought his first stock in 1941. He was a millionaire by 1960 and surpassed the $1billion mark in 1986. He has accumulated $19billion of his $86billion fortune in the last two years.

It's going to be a while before you see any feedback or results from any changes you make now.

When I replaced my "go to" lunch of beans on toast with a healthy green juice, I saw absolutely no effect on the first day or the second or the third. But 30 days on, you could *see* the difference. A year later, I looked like a different person.

There is always a delay between the routine change and the feedback. That's perfectly normal and is to be expected. Remember, you are the compound effect of every decision you've ever made and every action you've ever taken. Those tiny flakes – the little habits and routines that on their own seem so small and insignificant – yield massive snowballs when rolled down the hill of time.

Remember the 40-year example just now, where we turned £681 into a million quid? Let's see how that actually stacks up over the years:

Year	Total with interest
1	£817
5	£1,694
10	£4,216
15	£10,492
20	£26,107
25	£64,964
30	£161,653
35	£402,245
40	£1,000,914

Not much happens for the first decade or two. Yet look what happens once the momentum of the hill of time kicks in – more growth happens in the final year (£166,819) than the first 30 years combined.

Forty years to make £1million out of £681. That's pretty cool. How much longer do you think it would take to make another million? Less than four years.

Four years later, your "cool million" is now worth £2,075,496. Forty years for the first million. Four years for the second. It's true what they say. The first million really *is* the hardest.

Homework

Question: What one thing can you change today that will compound over time?

3. MORNINGS DON'T HAVE TO BE MIRACULOUS!

A few years ago, there was a book doing the rounds of all the business growth groups I was in. Just about everyone I knew was raving about this revolutionary idea and how it had changed their lives.

That book was *'The Miracle Morning'* by Hal Elrod.

Eager to see what all the fuss was about, I set about reading the book. Apologies to Hal, but I'm going to give away the main plotline of the book in a few words (look away dear reader if you don't want any spoilers): Get up early and make time for personal development.

Of course, there's a lot more to it than that, but that's the TL/DR version.

I thought it sounded brilliant and was a chance to try out a brand new routine. Get up at 5am, have a healthy breakfast, do some meditation, get some exercise, read some personal development, write some affirmations, spend quality time with the kids, and *then* start my working day.

Just one slight problem.

I'm not a morning person.

Let me rephrase that.

I am NOT a morning person.

You know how Garfield "doesn't like mornings"? Well, deprive Garfield of his coffee, multiply that by ten and *that's* how much of a morning person I'm not.

I only have to be *aware* that I need to get up early the next day and I find myself unable to sleep at night. Pre-children, I would happily work until 2am and sleep until 10am.

Now Hal wants me to get up at 5am?

Well, never one to admit defeat before he's started, I dutifully set my alarm for 5am the next day and attempted to go to sleep.

After a fitful night's sleep, broken only by the calculations I was constantly doing in my head (working out how long I had left before I had to get out of bed), the alarm sprang into action.

And so did I. I had to leap out of bed to try to turn the alarm off before it woke the whole bloody house up. I stumbled around in the dark (being careful not to turn the lights on in case it woke the whole bloody house up) and after a brief toe-stubbing on the bottom stair, managed to make it upstairs to the kitchen (yes, we have an upside-down house), where I was greeted by Jinx, our springer spaniel, who presumed that because I was there it must be time to get up and have breakfast.

Jinx started jumping around with delight, expecting a nice early breakfast, so I spent the next few minutes calming her down so that she didn't wake the whole bloody house up. I went to make myself a nice healthy smoothie for breakfast, popping some spinach, banana, chia seeds, almond milk and raspberries into the blender and...

Oh yes, better not use the blender in case I wake the whole bloody house up. Right, let's go in the living room and do my morning workout. Crikey, it's freezing in here! Note to self: make sure the heating's on at 5am tomorrow morning.

Got my workout plan here, let's start with some burpees. Oh no. That'll be too noisy. I could wake the whole bloody house up. Jumping jacks are out too. And mountain climbers.

Bloody hell.

Never mind, at least I can read some personal development in peace before...

"Daddy! What are you doing up this early?"

There goes that idea.

On the bright side, it does at least mean I can have breakfast with the family and spend some quality time with them. And it looks like my wife Sarah is going to join us too – even she's decided to get up a little earlier than usual to embrace the joys of the morning.

"What the hell are you doing? You've woken the whole bloody house up!"

Not quite embracing the joys of the morning then.

The four of us sit, bleary-eyed and stony-faced, around the breakfast table, absolutely shattered before we've even started the day, more stressed than we were when the alarm went off and in no way ready for the day ahead. The only thing we were ready for was to go back to bed.

There was just enough time to squeeze in some affirmations before the school run, so we decide to do them as a family:

"I am never getting up at 5am again."

"I am not a morning person."

"I am going back to bed."

What's wrong with the 8am club?

Why do we sleep at night and wake during the day? It's down to our circadian rhythm – the natural ebb and flow of hormones and chemicals that regulate our bodies. It's a primal instinct, harking back to when we were cavemen and cavewomen and didn't have the luxury of electric lighting and central heating.

When it got dark at 5pm in midwinter, there was very little point sitting in the dark until midnight before going to bed. As a tribe, we rose with the sunrise and retired to bed with the sunset.

As a tribe, we did. But as individuals, we didn't.

Imagine how vulnerable the tribe would be if the entire camp was asleep from sunset to sunrise. In midwinter, that could leave the entire camp completely unguarded from predators and rivals for up to 15 hours a day. That's a recipe for disaster and one that we humans evolved to counter.

Rather than all working to the same schedule, we evolved to follow one of three *different* circadian rhythms.

Some people became early birds – rising before dawn, and sleeping just after sunset.

Others became night owls – these guys would guard the camp through the dark of the night, hitting the sack just before dawn, and rising again around midday.

And another group fell somewhere in-between, waking later than the early birds but before the night owls, and heading to bed well before the night owls called it a night, but several hours after the early birds had turned in.

All three groups followed an almost identical circadian rhythm in terms of the length of their day, but their wake and rest times were staggered.

The early birds were out foraging while the night owls slept.

The night owls guarded the camp while the early birds got some shuteye.

The inbetweeners hunted during the middle of the day and covered the overlap between the other two groups, who worked and slept at opposite ends of the day.

Most of us still fall into one of these three circadian rhythms. Which one sounds most like you?

1. **The early bird.**
   You naturally wake up early with the sun or earlier in winter. Waking at 4am or 5am doesn't faze you in the slightest. You're in the gym by six, ready to start work by seven, and full of energy and vigour.

   You get your best work done in the morning and hit your peak around midday. You start to flag in late afternoon and are ready for bed by 9pm. You have no problem falling asleep.

2. **The night owl.**
   Mornings are for other people. Waking up before midday is hard for you.

   Your best work is done in the late evening. You hit your peak around 7pm. You'll rarely feel tired before midnight and it's often much later. You have a tendency to keep going until you do feel tired.

3. **The inbetweener.**
   You're woken by an alarm and usually hit the snooze button (especially if your alarm is set to go off before your "natural" wake time).

   You hit your peak in the middle of the day and do your best work in the late morning and very early afternoon. You're tired by late evening and hit the sack by 11pm. You may struggle to sleep as deeply as you'd like.

I'm an inbetweener. Left to my own devices, I'd naturally wake around 8.30am and head to bed by midnight. But, of course, I live in a world where different circadian rhythms aren't taken into account.

It's no good me rocking out of bed at 8.30am when I have to deliver the kids to school by 8.45am. That just doesn't work.

If you employ a night owl and tell them they have to be in the office by 9am every day, that's a recipe for disaster. Not only are they likely to oversleep and be late on a regular basis, but you're forcing them to do their most critical work during their least productive time of the day.

Similarly, you wouldn't ask an early bird to be a night watchman. That would be crazy.

Yet this is why people with different circadian rhythms fall out with each other – they assume that everyone else is just like them. "If I can get up at 5am, why can't you?"

Night owls are often called lazy because they're still in bed while the early birds and inbetweeners (the majority of people) have been up for hours. Yet those same "lazy" people are working till midnight or beyond, while everyone else clocked off hours earlier and are snoring soundly in their beds.

Early birds spend most of their productive time waiting for places to open and everyone else to wake up. They feel that you've wasted the day and are frustrated that you're just tumbling out of bed and making your first coffee, while they've been ready to get shit done from the crack of dawn.

As an inbetweener, the biggest problem I've found is I'm just an hour or so out of sync with "the norm". I'd naturally wake full of energy at 8.30am, yet I need to set an alarm to wake me an hour earlier. We're expected to work 9am to 5pm, yet I work better from 10am to 6pm. Dinner is served at 5pm? That's still the middle of the afternoon for me.

Thankfully, I've been able to design my businesses around my circadian rhythm. While I still have the school runs to attend to, I can at least schedule in my most important tasks for the time of day when I'm at my peak and have the highest amount of energy. For me, that's the period from 10am to midday.

I schedule in "stuff" – such as checking emails, dealing with paperwork, admin, unimportant calls and meetings – when my energy levels are dropping in late afternoon. When I need to bring my A-game, I always try to work *with* my inbetweener nature rather than fight it.

Next time you're on social media and see a post from the 5am brigade bragging about how they've been "building their dreams while you're still dreaming in your bed", you'll know that you're reading a post from an early bird. And if you're a night owl or an inbetweener, you can safely ignore that post knowing that it's just written by someone who is wired differently than you.

When night owl and mathematical physicist James Clerk Maxwell arrived at Cambridge University in 1850, he was told there was to be a compulsory 6am church service every day. His reply?

"Aye, I suppose I could stay up that late."

Get. More. Sleep.

What's the one thing that almost every small business owner could do to make their business more successful?

Put their prices up? Do more marketing? Introduce a new product line? Embrace social media? Hire more staff?

Yep, those can all help, depending on how well your business is already doing and where you want it to go. But I believe there's one thing that can help just about every business owner that all the gurus in the world don't tell you.

It's the closest thing there is to a magic bullet. And everyone's looking for the magic bullet.

The magic bullet is...

Get more sleep.

That's it? Go to bed earlier? I haven't got time to sleep! What difference is an extra bit of shut-eye going to make?

Quite a lot actually.

One of my health goals for last year was to improve my sleep routine. I was going on holiday with the family, so I downloaded an audiobook to listen to by the pool. It was *'Why We Sleep'* by Matthew Walker.

It's not a business book. It's 13-and-a-half hours long and I can sum up the entire book in just three words:

Get. More. Sleep.

But it was so impactful that it changed my mindset around sleep 180 degrees over those 13 hours and 31 minutes. Previously, sleep was an inconvenience that robbed me of precious hours when I could be building my empire or enjoying life.

Sleep is just dead time, isn't it?

Walker presents case study after case study that shows how sleep affects absolutely everything we do as humans – how we look, how we think, how we feel, how we act, how long we live, how easily our bodies repair, how we age, how we make decisions, how successful we are, and how happy we are.

I saw Gary Vaynerchuk speak in London a few years back and still remember the advice he gave one poor soul who reached out to him for help, as he was struggling to get his business off the ground while working a full-time job.

Gary Vee's advice to that man was to "sleep less".

That was it. His entire advice in a nutshell. Screw sleep. Sleep is for losers. Join the 5am club and hustle like me.

Hands down, one of the worst pieces of advice I've ever seen dished out and, after hearing Matthew Walker's studies, possibly one of the most dangerous.

When we skimp on sleep, our prefrontal cortex (the decision-making part of our brain) doesn't work as well. People who are sleep deprived (which is actually most of us!) make worse decisions.

They're more likely to take the easy path (hitting the snooze button, grabbing a doughnut, cutting corners) and don't even know they're doing it. Sleep-impaired people don't realise how it affects their performance.

Getting a "solid" six hours sleep a night for ten days in a row has been shown to cause the same decrease in performance, response time and decision-making ability as one night with zero sleep. A 400 per cent decrease. And that's getting six hours a night, every night – something I did for *years*!

People who sleep less tend to wake up hungrier the following day and tend to choose less healthy options. They crave carbs and sugar. The willpower that was there the previous day has all but vanished.

Not getting enough sleep has also been shown to contribute to higher rates of mortality, increased risk of cancer, diabetes, dementia, heart disease, and inflammation.

The study that really leapt out at me from Walker's book was the data around having a "little less sleep" as a one-off. You wouldn't think that just having one hour's less shut-eye on one solitary night would make any difference, would you?

Well, Walker went back through the data and looked at the number of deaths in the UK by heart attack every year for the last 15 years, broken down by day. And he found two stark revelations. For 14 out of the 15 years, a Monday in late March showed the highest rate of heart attack deaths.

And, by contrast, a Monday in late October every year presented the fewest number of deaths.

What were these dates that seemed to result in people keeling over and dropping dead or feeling fit as a fiddle? And why were they always on a Monday?

The answer was British Summer Time.

When the clocks go forward on the last Sunday in March, the entire country gets one hour's less sleep. The following day, emergency departments up and down the country are inundated with heart attack victims.

In October, the clocks go back. Everyone gets an extra hour in bed and 24 hours later, the cardiac surgeons are sat twiddling their thumbs.

Sleep deprivation is for interrogating terrorists, not for people who want to grow their business and actually be around to enjoy the fruits of their labour.

By now, you're probably thinking, "Well, I'll sleep more when the business is doing better". The paradox is, perhaps the business *would* be doing better if only you slept more.

If you were going to run a marathon, you'd understand the importance of a proper training routine, making sure that your nutrition and training plan was on point for weeks and months in advance. You'd do practice runs of varying distances, all leading up to the main event. You'd stretch. You'd take on plenty of fluids. You'd make sure your running shoes didn't have holes in them. And you'd probably get a good night's sleep the night before.

You wouldn't just rock up having done zero preparation after a late night partying, put one foot in front of the other and hope for the best, would you? And yet, that's exactly what many of us do when running our own businesses.

We burn the candle at both ends and hope for the best. Sleep is an inconvenience and one that robs us of time we could spend building our dreams instead of just dreaming.

We don't stop and think how much more effective we'd be after a full night's sleep, how every decision we make could be better, how we would have more energy to get more done, how every skill we possess could be improved and sharpened or how sleep is the magic bullet we've been looking for.

Imagine you're booked in to have an operation on your spine and you have a choice of two surgeons. They both have the same qualifications and the same level of expertise. They're almost identical in every way. Except one.

The first surgeon had eight hours' sleep last night, while the second "only needs" five hours and a couple of coffees.

Which surgeon do you let loose on your spine with a scalpel?

You're the surgeon in your business. Which version of you do you let loose on your business?

My morning routine

Here's my usual morning routine.

7.24am First alarm goes off (this "pre-wakes" me).

7.26am Second alarm goes off (this also acts as a back-up should the first alarm fail to go off).

7.30am Shower and dress.

7.45am Brew coffee, check status of children (eldest should be dressed for school, youngest may still be asleep), and prepare breakfast for children.

7.50am Serve breakfast to eldest. Let dogs out into garden. Blend coffee with grass-fed butter and MCT oil to make Bulletproof Coffee.

8.00am Wake youngest and prepare breakfast for him.

8.05am Prepare second breakfast for eldest (he's a growing boy!). Serve breakfast to youngest.

8.10am Clear breakfast plate from eldest. Send him away to clean teeth, brush hair, wash face, put shoes on and find jumpers, coats and bags, etc. for school.

8.15am	Clear breakfast plate from youngest. Send him away to get dressed, clean teeth, brush hair, wash face, put shoes on and find jumpers, coats and bags, etc. for school.
8.20am	Check weather forecast and locate coats and jumpers if needed.
8.25am	Announce "five-minute warning" to both kids that we'll be leaving for school. Ask Alexa to play a high tempo rock song at high volume. Drink Bulletproof Coffee.
8.30am	Leave house with kids, bags, coats, jumpers, PE kits, lunchboxes, water bottles, science projects and "golden time" toys. Drive to school.
8.35am	Arrive at parking spot. Chat with kids about what they're looking forward to that day.
8.40am	Walk to school.
8.45am	Drop off youngest.
8.46am	Drop off eldest. Walk back to car.
8.50am	Drive home.
8.55am	Make large mug of lemon and ginger tea, pour a litre of water and head to the home office.
9.00am	Fire up the laptop and start working on my ONE thing for the day (which is already planned the day before, and *the* single most important task of the day).

That sounds quite a specific, almost military routine. But because it's a routine that I've been following for a couple of years now (and have tweaked and amended over those years), I can now go through that routine on autopilot and, most importantly, so can the kids.

They know exactly what they should be doing at any time. Jack, my eldest, knows that as long as he's dressed by the time I come upstairs, he's free to play on the Xbox, watch YouTube, play with

LEGO or whatever. The youngest, Harry, knows that everything happens very quickly once we wake him up. Once he's eaten his breakfast, he knows that I'll say to him "teeth, hair, face, shoes" and off he goes.

When he first started school a few years ago, I dropped him off at the school gates and was greeted by a supply teacher who noticed that his hair was gelled and combed in a style. "I don't know how you find the time to style his hair," she said. "I barely have time to do my own!"

It was obvious to me of course. I didn't "find" the time to do it. I *made* the time. It was simply part of our normal morning routine. While Harry brushes his teeth, I comb his hair. It took me ten seconds every morning and happened on autopilot.

The morning routine doesn't matter

That is my routine, of course. It's personal to me and it works for *me*. You could try to copy my routine into your life and absolutely hate it. It could cause chaos. Your routine doesn't have to start at 7.24am or 5am or 6am. You should choose, ideally based on your circadian rhythm.

You may not have to (or want to) take your kids to school. You may want to hit the gym, get straight to work, meditate or read, do yoga, go for a run, make some phone calls, read the newspaper or meet friends for breakfast. Whatever you want to do, it's *your* routine.

The important thing isn't getting up at 5am (unless you're an early bird and you want to of course!), it is *having* a routine when you *do* wake up.

I remember when I was just starting out in business, I used to read the profile of a successful businessman or woman in the Sunday papers. The format was the same every week (hmm, where have I heard that before?) and was a day in the life of... whoever.

Every week, in just about every profile, their day would start in a very similar way.

"5am. Wake up. Coffee. Hit the gym."

"4.30am. Alarm goes off. Go for a run."

"4am. Got to wake up before everyone else does."

It seemed there was a clear pattern. That all these successful people got up at silly o'clock in the morning, did some exercise and were in the office by 6am or 7am.

Bugger.

As an inbetweener, I had no chance.

I now know that the important thing is having a morning routine, full-stop.

Not one that starts in the middle of the night and makes you look superhuman to readers of a Sunday newspaper, but one that works for you. A morning routine that does all the heavy lifting and sets you up in the best possible way to hit the ground running when you do land at your desk – even if it starts at 11am with "have a cup of coffee and watch TV". If that's what sets you up for a really productive, high-energy day, then go for it.

If you'd be happier setting your alarm for 4am, doing a kettlebell workout and being first in the office then good for you. It's your routine. You choose.

Sir Richard Branson gets up at 5.45am every morning, but Winston Churchill didn't get out of bed until 11am. President George W Bush was tucked up by 10pm every night, while his successor Barack Obama could often be found burning the midnight oil until 2am.

If you want new results, you need new routines. But they've got to work for *you*. Copying someone else's just isn't going to help you in the slightest. *The* routine doesn't matter. What matters is that you *have* a routine.

Homework

Question: What's your natural circadian rhythm?

Task: Try to do the following three things every day for the next week:

1. Go to bed 30 minutes earlier than usual.
2. Wake up at the same time every morning, including weekends.
3. Implement one positive change into either your bedtime or morning routine.

4. EASY, GOOD. EASY, GOOD. ROUTINES ARE EASY, GOOD.

I hate hard things. I hate complex. I hate layer upon layer of red tape (probably why it didn't work out for me as a civil servant!).

I watched the Leonardo DiCaprio film Inception once. It's a bloody good film and I thoroughly enjoyed it. But I've no idea what happened in 90 per cent of it and would struggle to recap the plotline for you right now. It was just too complex.

But I can still recite every line of Pulp Fiction word-for-word (anyone for a Big Kahuna Burger?).

Because I'm a lazy bugger, I avoid things that are hard. That could mean I just avoid certain things altogether – or I might see if I can make them *easy*.

For example, take our Ambitious. Lifestyle. Business. Podcast. Had we done the podcast "properly" when we launched in 2016, we'd have spent thousands of pounds on equipment. It would also have taken us weeks of training to learn how to use it all, we'd have spent ten hours prepping each week, and recorded three hours of audio to end up with each 40-minute episode. And each episode would then have been edited to within an inch of its life. Plus we'd have employed researchers, sound technicians, marketers, and committed to treating it as a full-time job.

Or I could've bought a £50 microphone from Amazon, turned it on, sat down with Jason and started yapping. Which is exactly what we did. We decided to record everything in one take and upload to Libsyn (a single platform that populates iTunes, Stitcher, Spotify, etc.).

In short, we made podcasting easy. And because it was easy, we stuck at it – even when we only had 20 subscribers after six months. If podcasting had been hard, we'd have given up. We'd have placed podcasting on the "too hard" pile.

Yet here we are now, a couple of years in and about to record our 60th episode. Yep, 60 episodes.

And even as we go along now, we're still finding ways to make it easier. We now batch the recordings to get three months' worth of episodes "in the can", rather than rushing to record each one individually at the last-minute. We have a sound engineer to polish up the quality. We get One Percent Club members on as guests so we know their stories inside-out and can delve deep into the whys and hows of their success.

We also ask one of our team to watch each episode before it goes live to spot any possible edits we've missed and to pull out the main learning points and quotable lines.

What have you put off doing because it's "too hard"?

It might be worth having a browse through your "too hard" pile and asking yourself a simple question: "What would this look like if it were easy?"

Like any good accountant, a nice easy-to-follow routine should make you (or save you) more money than it costs.

Who are ya? Who are ya?

When you change your routines, you don't just change *what* you do. You change *who* you are.

As Aristotle said, we are what we repeatedly do.

From 1994 to 2006, I was a smoker. The record books (if there were such a thing for smoking) would show that I had my first cigarette on something like July 20th 1994 and my final toke came on April 12th 2006.

Does that mean that I went to bed on July 19th 1994 a non-smoker and woke up the following morning as a smoker?

No, of course not. If you'd asked me on the fateful day that I took my very first drag whether I was now a smoker, I'd have laughed at you. Of course I wasn't a smoker. I'd just had one little cigarette.

Even two weeks later, I wouldn't have classed myself as a smoker. Sure, I'd had a couple every Friday and Saturday night, but I was still a non-smoker. That was who I was.

And then there's a blurry line somewhere between that "just a couple at the weekend" to 20 a day. From non-smoker to smoker. The change didn't happen overnight, it happened over time as *I* changed.

It was the same when I quit. I still classed myself as a smoker for several months afterwards, despite not partaking of a single puff. I was a smoker who hadn't had a cigarette for a few months.

Then, one day, the story changed in my head. "I'm a smoker who's trying to quit" became "I'm an ex-smoker" and then eventually "I don't smoke".

I changed. My routines changed months before, but it took an age for my thinking and realisation about who I was caught up.

The story you tell yourself and who you believe you are is half the battle.

I found giving up drinking really easy compared to giving up smoking. I believe that's because of the story I told myself about who I was. When I gave up smoking, I thought of myself as "a smoker who was trying to quit" for several months. Yet when I gave up drinking, I "didn't want to drink" from day one.

A person who doesn't want to drink finds it easy to say no to a drink. A smoker who is trying to quit is still a smoker and has to use willpower to say no.

I don't have to use willpower to say no to cigarettes now, because *who I am* has changed. I'm a non-smoker now. People who don't smoke don't want cigarettes. People who don't drink don't want to get drunk.

I haven't eaten at McDonald's for ten years or more, and my kids have never eaten there. I used to enjoy a quarter pounder with cheese at least once a week. But now, I can't think of anything less appetising.

What changed?

I did. I don't eat at McDonald's. That's just who I am now. McDonald's didn't change. I did.

What you repeatedly do (or don't do) makes you who you are.

When you change *who you are*, it makes creating and sticking to routines congruent to your goals much easier.

If your goal is to become healthy, ask yourself "is this the routine of a healthy person?"

If you want to be more productive, ask "is this what a productive person would be doing right now?"

If you want to be a better leader, ask "what would a great leader do in this situation?"

Every time you ask what the person you want to become would do and then model that behaviour, you inch one small step closer to becoming that person. To changing who you are.

You are what you repeatedly do. Do what the person you want to be would repeatedly do and you'll become them.

Monkey see, Monkey do

Every night at around 7pm I get "the look". No words are spoken, it's just implied. Taken as gospel. It's happening. Like some kind of magic telepathy has taken place. We are going for a walk.

My springer spaniel Jinx and I have this magic telepathy off to a fine art. She's deaf as a doorpost, so it's no use using words. She can read my body language to a tee though. No sooner have I finished my tea (or "dinner" if you're posh), than I get "the look".

If I head towards the front door at any time, I get "the look". Put my coat on? Well, "the look" will surely follow.

She looks for "intent" – the hints that I *might* want to take her out for a walk, such as heading for the front door, putting my shoes on, or picking up a coat. She's become world class at spotting the visual clues that help reinforce the daily routine of going for a walk.

Visual clues are a fantastic way of bedding in a new routine.

Want to go for a run every day? Leave your running shoes by the front door. Need to spend less time on Facebook? Install a news feed blocker that displays a "nothing to see here, get back to work" message every time you start looking for cat videos.

Want to journal first thing every day? Put your journal on top of your cornflake bowl the night before. Read five pages before bed? Leave your book on the pillow in the morning. Want to drink more water? Get a water bottle with a visual guide that shows how much you've drunk.

We all follow visual clues. "Mind your head". "This way up". "No entry".

Monkey see, monkey do.

If you want Monkey to do it, make sure Monkey sees it.

Bad monkey! Stop it!

What if you don't want Monkey to do, though? Well, you'd better make sure Monkey sees something else.

You can break existing habits by interrupting your usual routine with something *very* different. You could go to a different place, for instance. When I gave up drinking, I'd go to the gym at the same time I would normally have gone to the pub on a Friday afternoon.

You could also do a very different task in the same place. Say you want to break the habit of arriving home, collapsing on the sofa, and binge-watching Netflix for the rest of the day. Why not arrive home, collapse on the sofa with the people you love and talk to them about their day? Or collapse on the sofa with a book? Or do push-ups on the sofa? Or throw away the sofa?

You're looking to interrupt your usual pattern. You want to break the autonomy of the Computer that's running things on autopilot and make a small (or large) adjustment to the program.

How do you make people believe that the Statue of Liberty has disappeared? You show them something else.

In 1983, magician David Copperfield did just that on live TV. With a small audience on a stage in front of the Staten Island monument, Copperfield raised a curtain that blocked Lady Liberty from view.

And when the curtain dropped, she had indeed vanished.

Or, at least, that's what you saw.

Because you only saw what Copperfield wanted you to see. He wanted you to see the gap in the skyline where a 93-metre statue was mere seconds ago.

He didn't want you to see the statue hiding behind a pillar, having slowly rotated the stage 20 degrees to the right while the curtain was raised. He didn't want you to hear the stage rotating, so he played loud rock music.

David Copperfield fooled hundreds of millions of people all over the world with this illusion, by simply choosing what he wanted you to see (and what he made sure you didn't see).

You can use the same tactics to trick your brain into doing what *you* want.

A wardrobe full of grey T-shirts

Let's say you're going to a fancy dress party as Steve Jobs. What do you wear? Easy. White trainers, stonewashed jeans, black turtleneck, pair of round glasses.

What about Mark Zuckerberg? Very similar. Trainers and jeans again. This time with a grey T-shirt. Maybe add a grey hoodie if you're cold.

Donald Trump? Business suit. White shirt. Red tie and a "Make America Great Again" baseball cap to top it off.

Why would three billionaires like Jobs, Zuckerberg and Trump choose to wear the same thing every day? Essentially, a uniform?

There are a couple of reasons.

The first is pretty obvious – it creates a brand. If I were to put on a black turtleneck and a pair of round glasses, you'd instantly think of Steve Jobs and Apple.

Mark Zuckerberg is a pretty average looking guy. How does he stand out? By being "the guy who always wears a grey T-shirt".

And if you were running for the office of President of the United States of America, would you be happy to wear a "uniform" in public that screamed professional businessman working for the USA (Trump did occasionally substitute the red tie for a blue one, but was never seen without some combination of red, white and blue).

But beyond the brand-building, there's some scientific logic to their decisions.

Scientists believe that the anterior cingulate cortex (ACC) part of your brain is where your willpower and decision-making skills come from. Every day, the ACC wakes up full of energy, but every single time you make a decision or do something mentally taxing, you use a little bit of that energy. You can think of your ACC as "decision calories".

If you use up all those calories with hundreds of trivial decisions such as "what am I going to wear today?" or "what shall I have for lunch?" then the ACC stops working as well and your willpower runs out. When your willpower runs out, that's when you start making bad decisions.

Doughnuts and procrastination ahoy!

As we're talking science, who better to bring into the discussion than Albert Einstein, one of the earliest pioneers of "wearing the same clothes every day"?

Now I don't know if you're aware, but Albert Einstein was quite an intelligent chap. He was a theoretical physicist, famed for developing the theory of relativity, and is often talked about as being the father of modern science. He loved nothing better than solving a good puzzle and this required a great deal of the processing power contained within his brain.

It was only natural to Einstein that his brain would have limited processing power and that using said power on silly decisions like what to wear or what to have for lunch was a waste of time.

So he went out and bought a handful of identical grey suits, which he wore every day (one at a time, of course). Just like Zuckerberg has a wardrobe full of grey T-shirts, every time Einstein opened his wardrobe each morning he was faced with nothing but grey suits.

Nothing but grey suits = No trivial decisions to make.

No trivial decisions to make = No processing power wasted.

No processing power wasted = Full power of the brain available for important decisions.

Most of us waste our decisions on trivial matters such as what to wear, what to have for breakfast or who to vote for in Celebrity Paint Drying.

Finally, we're standing at the kettle using up the last of our decision calories agonising over whether to have tea or coffee, only to find when we get back to work that we've got no processing power left for the really big decisions.

Decisions like how we're going to build the most valuable company in the world (Jobs), how to get a billion people using our product (Zuckerberg), or how we're going to become the leader of the Free World (Trump).

Trump's predecessor, Barack Obama, also understood the impact of what we now call "decision fatigue". In a 2014 Vanity Fair interview, he said: "You'll see I wear only grey or blue suits. I'm trying to pare down decisions. I don't want to make decisions about what I'm eating or wearing, because I have too many other decisions to make."

Good enough for two US Presidents. Good enough for the creator of the world's largest social network. Good enough for the creator of the iPhone. Good enough for you?

Riddle me this...

It's 3am and the doorbell goes. You wake, startled and not a little alarmed. Who could it be at this time of night?

It's your parents. They decided to pop in and surprise you and join you for breakfast. They must have heard about this 5am club thing and decided to get there early.

You let them in and look in the fridge, then the cupboard. You've got some breakfast options – strawberry jam, honey, a jar of coffee, and a bag of doughnuts.

What do you open first? The coffee? The jam jar?

No, it must be the fridge. You opened that before the cupboard.

But how did your parents get in the house? The front door, of course! That was the first thing you opened.

Wrong.

The very first thing you opened, at 3am, without even thinking about it?

Your eyes.

That happened completely on autopilot. You didn't need to expend any conscious effort whatsoever to open your eyes. It just happened. So subconsciously that most people who read this riddle completely overlook it.

It just happens.

When was the last time you remember blinking? I mean, actually consciously remember blinking? Unless you've had something in your eye, conjunctivitis or put contacts in recently, I'm betting it's been a few hundred thousand blinks since you noticed one.

And now that I've mentioned it, I've brought it to your attention and you've probably noticed the last few blinks. Don't worry, you can go back to blinking on autopilot soon – you just need to stop thinking about it.

If you can get your routines to "blinking level" – where they just happen automatically, without any conscious effort from you – that's the sweet spot. You've programmed the Computer and it can just run the script again and again.

<blink>

<eat a healthy breakfast>

<blink>

<read five pages of a book>

<blink>

<pick up the phone and make a sales call>

<blink>

<go for a run>

<blink>

<tell someone you love them>

<blink>

To begin with, you're going to have to consciously run these scripts yourself as the Human is still in charge. But when you've done the same thing over and over and over again, your Computer will create a script to run on autopilot for you and file that script alongside blinking, breathing and brushing your teeth.

So how do we get the Computer to create that script?

Sticky the stick insect stuck on a sticky bun

We all go into things with the best of intentions. Visit any gym in January for a visual demonstration. But how do we actually stick at it when things get hard and our motivation wanes?

We need a routine that is as easy to stick to as Sticky the stick insect stuck on a sticky bun.

Matt, one of our One Percenters, was a serial procrastinator. He'd be really busy for most of his working day, but he'd be forever working on the wrong things.

He'd be playing around with the colour scheme of his website rather than working on his Google ads. He'd tidy the office rather than look at his accounts. Get his inbox to zero rather than do lead generation work.

And he was struggling big time. During one of our coaching calls, he confessed: "I need to earn money, pronto."

To an outsider, the answer was obvious. He needed to do more of the stuff that actually *earns* money and stop doing the stuff that doesn't. If you want different results, you need different routines.

Matt had two objections to that answer:

1. He was already really busy, doing all the stuff that earned no money.
2. He enjoyed doing the things that earned no money and didn't enjoy the money-making stuff.

In other words, Matt was quite happy in his current comfort zone. He was doing things that he enjoyed and avoided things that were too hard. Unfortunately, the things in Matt's current comfort zone weren't paying the bills.

Now, unless Matt wants to register as an official charity, let's assume that he's in business because he wants to earn a living. He wants to provide for his family and earn every penny.

In order to do that, he's going to need to step outside of his comfort zone.

I often talk about comfort zones using the analogy of a hula hoop. The smaller your hula hoop, the smaller your comfort zone. When you do things that are *just* outside of the hoop, just outside of your comfort zone, your hula hoop gets bigger and what was scary just now, is not anymore.

We're scared of the unknown. Everything's scary until you've done it.

What else was scaring Matt from taking the right actions?

The vast expanse outside of the hula hoop. He'd stand inside that tiny circle and see others spending £30,000 a month on Facebook Ads, employing a team of sales staff or borrowing £100,000 to finance a new project. That scared the hell out of him. But he was inside a small hula hoop, looking at what others were doing five miles away. He was comparing page four of his book with page 324 of someone else's.

So we created a simple routine for him.

Matt had to perform one task per day that either directly resulted in sales or had serious potential to lead to sales. He didn't have to blow £30k on Facebook Ads, but why not spend £5 a day testing them out and learn how they work?

Do income-producing work every day that's just outside of your comfort zone. Every day.

And it was the "every day" where Matt fell down.

He'd jump on a One Percent Club coaching call on the Monday, get all fired up and do great income-producing work on the Tuesday and Wednesday. But by the next time we'd chat, it had fallen by the wayside and he'd reverted to his old ways.

He'd shrunk back into his hula hoop. The Monkey had taken control again before the Human had a chance to program the Computer.

During one coaching call, we spotted that Matt had a planner on the office wall behind his desk. So we gave him some homework.

"Go out and buy some sticky dots."

One trip to the local office supplies store later and, armed with 200 bright green sticky dots, Matt was ready to rock and roll. His instructions were simple:

"Every day, do one piece of income-producing work that's just outside of your comfort zone, even if it's only for five minutes. And when you're done, stick a green dot on your wall planner for that day."

For the first few days, it seemed pointless. Matt isn't a four-year-old. He doesn't need a star chart for eating his vegetables or not wetting the bed. But the principles are the same. The four-year-old gets ten stars on her chart and earns a Frozen DVD. She gets 25 stars and it's a trip to the zoo.

Matt can also reward himself. Five green dots will get him a Starbucks. Ten is lunch at his favourite restaurant. Twenty-five gets him a weekend break with the family (or *from* the family if that motivates him more!).

And what does Matt get for using all 200 green dots? A business that's in a much better place and earning a lot more money. And that's not all, because Matt has changed who he is over those 200 dots. His hula hoop is much bigger than it was a year ago. He's now got the skills that pay the bills. He'll have those skills for the rest of his life and all it cost him was a pack of green sticky dots.

Those green sticky dots created the chain reaction that kept Matt going. Once you've got six, seven or eight green dots in a row, you don't want to break the chain.

And what if you *do* fall off the wagon and break the chain? You get back on the damn horse and start a new chain, that's what. Winners don't wallow in self-pity and give up. They develop bouncebackability. They start a new chain and aim to beat their previous PB.

I once did a 28-day HIIT workout challenge. Now, I'm no stranger to exercise, but my go-to routine that the Computer runs for me is "go to the gym twice a week", so actually working out every single day for four weeks straight was a real challenge for me.

I printed off a sheet of A4 that looked like an advent calendar. It had all the days listed, one to 28, with the corresponding exercises for each day in each "window".

Day one was easy. I put a big X through the day one window with a permanent marker. Days two, three and four were a breeze. Three more Xs were added.

And then the aching started. I'd have quite liked to skip day five but I didn't want to break the chain, so I soldiered on. It was only for ten minutes anyway. Another X in the box.

After a few weeks, I had to go to Birmingham for a few days and was living out of a hotel. That sheet of A4 came with me and I ensured that I put my Xs in the box every single day, even if it meant setting the alarm for 20 minutes earlier in the morning or slipping away at lunchtime to go and do some burpees in my hotel room.

My focus by now wasn't on the results I was going to get by doing the exercise, how much better I felt or the endorphins flowing through my body. No, my motivation was simply to get a full house of Xs in all 28 boxes. To complete the set and not break the chain.

I was that four-year-old, again, who *really* wanted a train set.

Whether you use red Xs, green dots or sparkly stars, anything you can do to start that chain reaction will help the Human brain create the pattern so that the Computer can write the script. Choose your reward and embrace your inner four-year-old.

Do the work. Get the reward.

Maybe you feel a bit stupid about it, but do it anyway. Then do the same thing tomorrow. And the next day. And the next. Build up that streak. Every day your growth compounds. Do it every day for two years and your life will be completely different.

The knee bone's connected to the thigh bone

Once a routine is established, you can start to connect others to it. Everything has an order. You wake up, go to the toilet, brush your teeth, shower, dress, etc. There's an order to all of it.

Imagine I want to add a new routine of flossing my teeth before bed every night. If I need to randomly remember to do this brand new routine, which I've been successfully *not* doing for the last four decades, I'm going to need some help.

The first thing I'm going to do is add a visual reminder. So I'm going to take one single floss stick and leave it on the bathroom shelf (which is at eye-level for me). I do this once.

Now, I look at my current bedtime routine. Turn off screens, have sauna, shower, feed dogs, read, lights out.

There are a couple of places that this new habit could fit into my current routine. The most obvious would be either before or after the shower. However, trial and error told me that this wasn't working as it just wasn't latching onto the current setup and it was getting missed.

So I moved it to immediately before having my sauna. I created a new rule that I can't have a sauna (reward) unless I've also got minty-fresh breath from having cleaned my teeth. And what do I do immediately before brushing my teeth? I floss. And then I take the next day's floss stick out of the pack and put it into place as a visual clue for tomorrow.

When trying to establish a new routine, look for something you already do, something that's already being run on autopilot, to which you can attach it. Just be aware that you will need to use a pattern interrupt with a visual clue to force the Computer to spot there's been some tweak to the code in this particular routine.

We just decided to go

What's the hardest part about going for a run? Is it the aching afterwards? The tightness in your chest as you tire? Getting a stitch? Your lack of stamina? Your jelly legs on hills? The time it takes to warm up, do the run and warm down?

Nope.

The hardest part of going for a run, the one thing that stops most people from running, is lacing up your trainers.

Once your running shoes are on and tied, you're *going* to head out the door. You're *going* to warm up. You're *going* to push yourself. You're *going* to do this.

In the film Apollo 13, Jim Lovell (played by Tom Hanks) watches Neil Armstrong and Buzz Aldrin land on the surface of the Moon in July 1969 and says: "From now on, we live in a world where

Man has walked on the Moon. And it's not a miracle, we just decided to go."

They just decided to go.

That's the hard part. Deciding to go. Deciding to do.

Deciding to do is the tipping point. I'm talking about *truly* deciding, making an absolute and unbreakable contract with yourself that says, "*We are doing this.*"

Lacing up those trainers. Signing that contract. Publicly stating you're going to write a book.

That last one is what I did in the summer of 2018, a year after my first book hit the bookshelves and after I had declared many, many times that I would never write another book again.

But this idea kept niggling at me. All the success I've had and all the success I witness, so much of it comes down to routine – to simply doing the right things, day in and day out.

Geoff Woods made his "King of Routine" comment and I found it harder and harder to resist the temptation to write another book. I needed to get off the fence and either *do* this or bury the idea forever.

I'm not the sort of person who can keep an idea "on ice" for any length of time. As Yoda may (or, more likely, may not) say, "Do or do not. There is no 'maybe one day'."

We had a family holiday booked for the summer – a fortnight in the sun with no work and zero responsibilities. I decided to use this downtime away from the hustle and bustle of everyday business life (obviously I don't allow a great deal of hustle or bustle in my everyday life anyway!) and took my journal with me.

My theory was thus: if I had a book in me, I'd be able to jot down loads of ideas. If I struggled to write down the basic chapter outline for this book, then I would consign the idea to the dustbin, never to see the light of day.

After 90 minutes (and three cappuccinos) sat by the pool, I'd noted down almost 100 ideas. I'd filled page after page after page in my journal.

Ping!

Imagine a lightbulb going off above my head at this exact moment, for this is the exact moment that it happened.

I *decided.*

I decided to write this book at that exact moment, sat by a swimming pool in Corfu with my fourth cappuccino next to me and the kids splashing in the pool.

The one thing I needed to do next was to commit – to lace my trainers – and give myself some public accountability.

So I took out my phone and went live on Facebook to our Ambitious. Lifestyle. Business. Community. The title of my live video was: "I might possibly have decided to write book #2..."

Of course, there was no "possibly" about it. Do or do not. My trainers were laced. It was several months before I wrote a single word of this book and almost a year before it became the finished article that you hold in your hands right now. But I took action immediately.

Decide to go and put your trainers on. The rest will follow.

One of my mentors used to preach about "reducing the time between the idea and the implementation". This is advice that has served me well over the years. I don't have half-baked ideas floating around the place, unfinished.

I have an idea and I do it or I decide not to do it.

But either way, I decide and I act immediately after deciding. I take the very first step towards achieving my goal or I ditch the idea, never to be seen again.

Can you do one press-up?

In her 2014 book *'The First 20 Minutes'*, American journalist Gretchen Reynolds lays out the groundwork for the most effective exercise regime for the majority of the population. The secret is in the title – it's those first 20 minutes that deliver the biggest bang for your buck.

Once you get past the 20-minute mark, you are still getting results but the return on investment (the benefits you get out for the effort you're putting in) starts slowing considerably. Running for 40 minutes is better than running for 30 minutes, but not by much. Whereas running for 15 minutes gives a much higher ROI than five minutes.

But what gives you by far *the* biggest increase in ROI?

From zero to one. From off to on. From sat on the couch to trainers laced and heading out the door.

If you're looking for the "minimum effective dose" of exercise, then this is it – do *something* every day. It doesn't matter what. Just be active. Find something you enjoy. Go from zero to one, and momentum will do the rest.

You never have to go past 20 minutes if you don't want to, as you know the returns are going to slow from then and you want the biggest bang for your buck.

You can apply the same principles to any goal you want to achieve. Want to read more? Go from zero to one. Read one page every day or one line! Want to make more sales calls? Pick up the phone every day. From zero to one. Trying to learn a new language? Learn one new word or phrase per day. Zero to one. Looking to improve your golf swing? Hit one ball a day. Zero to one.

You're unlikely to stop at one, but you've got your trainers laced and you're out the front door. Momentum will take you the rest of the way. You know that you can stop after 20 minutes (or 20 calls, or 20 pages, or 20 golf swings) before the ROI starts slowing down and your motivation wanes.

Save your energy for another 20 minutes tomorrow.

Jason and I were talking about breaking down massive scary goals into bite-size chunks on the Ambitious. Lifestyle. Business. Podcast a while back and I happened to mention a press-up challenge that I'd done the month before.

"I can't do press-ups," Jason said.

"That's not true," I immediately replied. "I bet you can."

"Nope, I've never been able to do them. Hated them at school."

"Could you do *one*?"

"Yeah, probably. But that would be my limit."

"So do one. Then stop. Then do one again tomorrow. And one the day after. One more the day after that. Once you've been doing one a day for a week, you might feel like trying a second. Then do two a day until you feel like trying three."

Jason was put off press-ups by the sheer size of the gap. He was currently doing zero and thought that "doing press-ups" meant doing 20 or 30 at a time. When we reduced the gap from zero to one, it stopped being scary. Of course he could do one lousy press-up.

That was two years ago, and Jason is now able to do sets of 500 one-armed press-ups with a small child sat on his back. Or maybe not, but I'm sure he could manage three or four press-ups now before he goes purple in the face and collapses in a heap.

What would this look like if it were hard?

Throughout this chapter, we've looked at the various ways you can make creating and sticking to positive new routines as easy as possible. Now let's flip that on its head.

How can we make negative routines as hard to follow as possible? Those routines that are already ingrained after years and years of following the script that the Monkey wrote for us. Those routines that have already reached blinking level of unconscious automation.

Picking up a McDonald's on the way home from work. Checking your phone every time it buzzes. Spending 80 per cent of your day in your inbox. Taking the lift rather than the stairs.

Your routines are either working for you or against you. Adding new routines that work for you can absolutely change your life. But often removing (or amending) the routines that are currently working against you can have just as big an impact, especially once you've rolled that routine down the hill of time.

If making a new habit stick like Sticky the stick insect stuck on a sticky bun is a matter of reducing friction, having visual reminders to take action and creating a chain reaction that results in a reward, then it stands to reason that the best way to make a bad routine less likely to stick around is to do the opposite.

1. **Create more friction:** Lock your phone in a drawer or turn it off when you're supposed to be working. Add additional passwords to those apps and websites that suck your time away.

2. **Remove visual reminders:** Delete the Facebook app from your phone. Drive a different route so you don't go past McDonald's. Shut down your inbox unless you're consciously working in there.
3. **Create a chain reaction for not following the bad routine:** Give up smoking by not having a cigarette today. Give yourself a sticker. Do the same again tomorrow. And the day after. Ten stickers equals a small reward, 30 stickers equals a bigger reward and 200 stickers equals you being a non-smoker.

Go through your home now and look at your current setup. Is it making the good routines easier or the bad routines?

Do you have takeaway menus on the fridge? I replaced mine with a photo of me when I was fat. Now every time I go to the fridge to binge and satisfy Monkey cravings, I get a visual reminder to eat healthily (or at least exercise portion control).

What's on the arm of your favourite comfy chair? Is it the TV remote or your current reading book? Are your running shoes or your slippers next to the front door?

I fell into the habit of working late into the evening and just about every weekend while writing '*Big Ideas...*'. I know, how ironic. Writing a book about lifestyle businesses while burning the candle at both ends!

One simple change put a stop to that. I set the heating in my office to turn off at 5pm every day and not to come on at all at weekends. That made it harder for me to work in the evenings and at weekends. Not impossible, of course. If I really needed to work, I could pop a jumper on and turn the heating up manually.

But there was just enough friction to awaken the Human and remind the Computer. "Oh yeah, I'm not supposed to be working now!"

Want to make sure you're in bed by 10pm every night? Make it hard not to be. Set timers so that the electricity is cut to the TV, the wifi and maybe even the lights to everywhere but the bedroom from 9.55pm.

For every single negative routine you want to change, just ask yourself this question: "What would this look like if it were hard?"

Homework

Question: How can you make your positive routines easy?

Question: How can you make your negative routines hard?

Task: Do something today to go from zero to one. Decide to go. Decide to do. Lace up your trainers and walk out the front door.

5. JOHN'S MARVELLOUS MEDICINE

In my first book, I laid out what I believe to be the five magic ingredients for success. Whether you're looking at Elon Musk aiming to colonise Mars or your child taking their first steps, you can bet your bottom dollar that at least three or four of these ingredients were present.

The more you can line up, the better your chances. Remember, everything compounds!

These five ingredients made such an impact on my life that I had them painted in foot-high letters on my home office wall. They act as a daily reminder for me. When I'm not achieving the success I would like or when it feels like I'm pushing treacle uphill, I know I'm probably missing an ingredient or two.

It's like how a good chef can take a small taste of a dish and automatically know what's missing. They know what the dish needs to bring it to life and how a dash of basil, a splash of white wine or a little more salt can achieve near-perfection.

Once you learn these five ingredients, you'll know exactly what's missing in your quest for success. As I said in '*Big Ideas...*': "Every single one of these 'magic ingredients' actually contains no 'magic' at all. They're just routines, habits and characteristics that your average, everyday, bog-standard human can use to appear super-human. And they're the building blocks on which I've built my businesses over the last two decades."

So, let's dip our finger into the pan and see what ingredients our Routine Risotto is made up of, shall we?

Ingredient #1 – Goals

You'd be hard pressed to find a kitchen without salt and pepper to hand and well-defined goals are a similar staple ingredient of any successful routine. Very few people achieve success by accident. Unless this is the very first personal development book you've picked up (welcome to the world of self-improvement if it is), then you'll have heard all about the importance of setting goals many, many times before. I won't bore you with all the scientific and anecdotal evidence.

Just know this: setting goals makes you more likely to achieve them. Writing them down makes it even more likely. And you can improve your chances further still by sharing those goals publicly and asking to be held accountable to them.

In the next chapter, once you've learnt all five magic ingredients, I'll share with you the system that I've used for the last five years to plot out and achieve some massive goals by breaking them down into small baby steps and simple daily routines.

But before you start setting yourself big, scary-arsed, routine-based goals, let's pause and think about what you actually want to achieve.

You could set a routine to go to bed 30 minutes earlier. But why?

You could make every Monday "meat-free Monday". But why?

You could read ten pages of a non-fiction book every day. But why?

Too many people plan their routine goals based on what they're going to do, not what they want to achieve by doing it. They see someone post on Facebook about getting up at 5am every day and think they'll give it a go too.

There are nine reasons why humans are driven to take action and if you focus on what you actually want rather than just setting goals based on what your Facebook friends are doing, you'll find sticking to the routine much, much easier.

So, by all means, have some goals in mind, but first let's just check that those goals are what you really, really want, shall we?

Ingredient #2 – Desire

"He who has a why can bear almost any how," says Viktor Frankl in his book *'Man's Search for Meaning'*, which chronicles his years spent in a Nazi concentration camp during World War II.

Simon Sinek tells us that "people don't buy what you do; they buy why you do it".

William Barclay believed "there are two great days in a person's life – the day we are born and the day we discover why".

It's fair to say, therefore, that the *why* matters every bit as much as the what. Maybe more so.

I mentioned just now that there are nine reasons that persuade us to take action, whether that's to get our credit card out and buy something, to commit to a course of action, or to start, stop or tweak a current routine.

Those whys are:

1. To be healthy or healthier!
2. To be popular – to impress people.
3. To be more attractive.
4. To have more meaningful relationships.
5. To have more security.
6. To make things easier.
7. To have more free time.
8. To achieve fulfilment.
9. To have more money.

Now, I would argue that ninth reason could be drilled down further to *why* do you want more money? Is it so that you'll have more security? To impress people? To feel fulfilled? To buy things for your kids? To spend on your health?

I don't believe that "to have more money" is the real reason. Yet it's often the first place that people start when setting goals: "I want to make £1million next year."

OK. But why?

There's nothing wrong with setting a nice big monetary goal like the magic million, as long as you know the *real reason* you want it. If being a millionaire matters to you so that you can stick two fingers up to the people who bullied you at school, fair play. Just be honest about it and realise that flicking vees at the bullies is your *true* desire and not six zeros on your bank statement.

Because, unless you've got a true burning desire for one of the reasons above, £1,000,000 is just that – six zeros. "000,000".

"He's in Resus."

Those three words filled me with dread. My youngest son Harry had been taken to hospital via ambulance after vomiting and fainting at home. My wife Sarah travelled in the ambulance with Harry and I drove up separately.

I arrived at A&E a few minutes behind the ambulance (they wouldn't let me drive through red lights or blast other cars out of my way in traffic) and asked where Harry was. The receptionist gave me some instructions that involved left turns, doors, right turns, corridors and one-way systems.

Needless to say, I got lost and ended up in the main action area of the emergency department of our local hospital. It might only have been midday on a Saturday lunchtime, but Saturday morning is clearly the peak time for injuring yourself. All those DIY accidents, football injuries, domestics and still-drunk-at-

9am-punch-ups. It was like the green room for extras on the set of the Walking Dead.

I managed to grab the attention of the nurse who looked like they were spinning the fewest plates (they were probably just starting their latest 20-hour shift), apologised for intruding and asked where I might be able to find my son.

Nurse One shouted across the room to Nurse Two: "Harry Lamerton?"

Nurse Two types into the computer.

"He's in resus."

What? What the actual f***? That would be "resus" as in "resuscitation"? The "resus" I've seen on TV dramas where they get the electric paddles out, yell "clear" a few times and then announce the time of death?

"Wait there a minute, Sir."

Nurse Two disappeared into a room with a big red sign above the door that read: "Resuscitation Unit. No admittance to unauthorised personnel."

I was left alone for around 90 seconds.

A minute and a half not knowing what had happened to my child, and fearing the worst. Staring at that sign, playing those old "time of death" scenes in a loop in my head and trying to figure out what the hell happened on the way to the hospital.

What do you think happened to all my goals in those 90 seconds?

Yep, they completely vanished. Making a million pounds? Not interested. Losing a bunch of weight? Couldn't care less.

Booking a ski holiday for next year or improving my golf game? Whatever. There was only one thing that I *truly* desired in those 90 seconds and it was for Harry to be OK.

Nurse Two led me into resus and I walked past people who were having a worse day than my boy. Past the heart attack and stab victims, at the very end of the room, was Harry looking very sorry for himself and attached to all sorts of machines. But very much alive and, thankfully, in no need of any resuscitation.

Twelve hours later, he was discharged and left the hospital with a diagnosis of gastric flu and two very relieved parents.

Thanks to that little event, I now have a desire meter to which I can compare my goals.

Wanting Harry to be OK rates 100 on the desire scale. Going back to my day job as a civil servant is a zero.

The more I really, *truly* desire something, the more likely I am to actually do the work necessary to get it.

I'd quite like a Ferrari 458 Italia. But that's the problem. It's something I'd *quite like*. It's not something I *truly* desire. It's probably a 15 on the desire scale.

But taking the family on a ski trip next year? That's more like an 85 on the desire scale. It occupies my thoughts on a regular basis and ensures that I'm always taking action to move me towards that goal – signing up for ski holiday alerts, booking dry slope lessons and getting feedback from others who have done it. There's a bloody good chance it'll happen.

Because I want it bad enough. I've decided to go.

Ingredient #3 – Knowledge

Remember how Samwell Tarly defeated the "incurable" Greyscale disease in Game of Thrones? Yep, he "read the book and followed the instructions".

Sam identified a knowledge gap between what he currently knew and what he needed to know. And he filled it. The montage on the television programme might only have taken a couple of minutes, but you can be sure he would have spent days upon days poring over heavy textbooks and medical encyclopaedias to close that knowledge gap inch by inch until he'd achieved what the wise elders could not.

Charlie Munger tells us how he's amassed nearly two billion dollars by constantly narrowing his knowledge gap: "Spend each day trying to be a little wiser than you were when you woke up."

There are very few better ways to guarantee success than to be constantly learning.

What's your current knowledge routine? Do you read ten pages of non-fiction every day? Listen to podcasts instead of the radio every time you get in the car? Audiobooks while walking the dog? Could you replace a current routine that isn't closing your knowledge gap with one that does?

Watch a TED Talk instead of scrolling through Facebook for 13 minutes. Read a blog post instead of watching Corrie.

You don't know what you don't know. By adding routines that narrow your knowledge gap, you will become a lifelong student – a persistent learner.

You'll become someone who reads the books and follows the instructions. With an estimated 140million books in the world, that's a lot of books to read and a lot of instructions to follow.

So if you want to know how to grow your business, invest in the stock market, become a better golfer, lose weight, learn to speak

Cantonese, find out what made Winston Churchill tick, discover everything you ever wanted to know about slugs and snails, or read the story of the man who mistook his wife for a hat, there's a book out there for you.

(Yes, that last one is a real book.)

Ingredient #4 – Environment

I didn't particularly enjoy the writing process for my first book and that was almost entirely down to the environment that I was writing in. I'd given myself a public deadline (see public accountability, under magic ingredient #1) and then had to work like a madman to meet that deadline while also juggling everything else I was doing to run our businesses.

Never mind spinning plates, I was busy juggling them! So I'd try to *squeeze in* an hour of writing here or a half day there. Just as I got into my flow, it was time to stop. And then it got to breaking point where the only way I was going to meet my (self-imposed) deadline was to drop everything and just write full-time.

I got it done and, dare I blow my own trumpet a little, I think I did a bloody good job. But I didn't really enjoy the process. So much so that on stage at the official launch party I proudly announced: "I'm never writing another book again!"

Yeah, that worked out well.

As soon as I decided to write Routine Machine, I was determined to actually enjoy writing it. I knew I needed to tweak my book-writing routine to affect my environment. Writing had to be a pleasure, not a chore. Something to be enjoyed, not endured.

The first thing that had to go was this ridiculous "an hour here, half a day there" setup. So I blocked an entire week out of my calendar. Everything else was cancelled or moved.

All of my team knew not to disturb me, upon penalty of death. I even posted in our Facebook community with a simple message for all of our clients: "F*** off, I'm writing!"

I turned on my email autoresponder for the first time in years with a simple message: "I'm not here. Back next week."

My phone was turned to silent and I ensured that I had the house to myself. No interruptions. Peace and quiet.

I wrote the first 31,000 words of this book in that first week. That's nearly half the book!

It was the very first draft, so it was really rough work. There was some very ropey writing (what do you mean "there still is"?), and much of what was written that week has not made it into this final version. But it broke the back of what looked like a mammoth task and it gave me a huge amount of momentum – momentum that I carried forward by blocking out three-day chunks of my calendar every month for the following six months.

I didn't pick up the book at all between those monthly sessions, but during the 18 days I had blocked out I focused exclusively on writing to the detriment of everything else.

Or at least, that was the plan.

Month two, and Sarah was home ill from work for two out of the three days. Just having someone else in the house changed my environment a tiny fraction, but it made it so much harder for me to actually concentrate and get into the "flow".

Even though she mostly kept out of my way (she did pop her head into the office once, only to have it bitten off by a frustrated would-be author who had "all the right words, but not necessarily in the right order") and I worked with the door shut, I'd hear her downstairs watching some TV show with a load of shooting and car chases, whereas my usual writing environment is to play a repetitive song on repeat on a low volume. (My go-to song for this is *'Time'* by Hans Zimmer from the Inception soundtrack.)

Month one: 31,000 words.

Month two: 14,000 words.

You can clearly see the impact that one subtle change in my environment had on me. I was less than half as effective.

It was exactly the same when we used to have a couple of physical offices. I hated working in them as I was never as effective as I was sat on my own at home. Someone would always pop their head around the corner to ask a quick question, get my thoughts on something or just say "hello".

And what happened every time they did?

I stopped what I was doing. And then I had to start up again. It would take me ten minutes just to get back into the groove, by which point some other bugger would interrupt me.

Have a look around your working environment right now. How easy is it for someone to interrupt you or stop you from working on what you should be doing?

When was the last time you had a whole week or a whole day without interruptions? Or even a few hours? What do you *allow* to be part of your daily routine that needs to change?

I now have my set writing routine that I can just turn on – house empty, phone off, emails off, all browsers closed, *'Time'* playing on a loop, just me and the book. Arse in seat, hands on keyboard.

And you know what? I'm enjoying the process of writing this book.

Or at least I was.

The kids are home from school now, so I've got Minecraft blaring outside my office door, both kids running around after the puppy and Harry's just wandered into my office mid-sentence to ask for a juice. Might be time to put the pen down until I can get the environment right again!

(One of the best ways to change your environment is to change who you hang around with. Why not hang around with hundreds of fellow Routine Machines, in a private Facebook community, which I created exclusively for readers of this book? You'll find a link to the Facebook group in the resources section at the end of the book.)

Your fellow Routine Machines can hold you accountable, inspire you, help you establish those new routines, and keep streaks going on existing ones. Who you hang around with really does matter - if you want better results, you need better friends!

Ingredient #5 – ACTION!

People who *do* more, achieve more. They fail more and they succeed more. Don't worry, I've not converted to the hustle brigade and I'm not going to tell you to JFDI. I'm a firm believer in going 100mph in the *right* direction and that means taking some time to evaluate which might be the right direction.

But sooner or later, you've gotta decide and you've gotta take some ACTION!

This is the only magic ingredient that warrants not only capital letters, but also an exclamation mark. That's how crucial it is.

Because no matter what your goals are, no matter how badly you desire them, how much knowledge you acquire or how much you fine-tune your environment, if you don't get off your arse and *do* something then you'll never get to where you want to go.

You can be the kid at the top of the death slide, looking down and having this conversation with yourself: "This is higher than I thought...I might go after this next boy's been down...Wow, he went fast. That's scary...What if I skin my arms?"

Or you can be the kid at the top of the death slide, looking down and having the following conversation with yourself: "3, 2, 1... Wheeeeeeee!!!!"

The first kid is having a conversation with his Monkey.

The Monkey wants to keep him safe, so he's screeching at the top of his lungs: "Danger! Danger! This is scary! Falling from heights is bad. Falling fast is bad. Falling fast from heights is really bad! Danger! Danger!"

Now the kid knows it's safe really, but he's entered into a conversation with the Monkey.

Here's a routine that can turn you into an action-taker: Never talk to Monkeys.

There are several ways you can do this. The easiest is to cut down the time between the idea and the implementation.

"I fancy going down that death slide" = go down the death slide.

Not, "I *think* I fancy going down that death slide. Do I? I think so. It does look quite high. Let me go up and have a little look."

Think it. Do it.

And if that Monkey starts piping up, you can turn him off by asking the Computer to run a pre-programmed script.

Remember the TV show Gladiators? That Saturday night staple of 90s TV where normal people like Adrian, from Basingstoke, and Susan, from Watford, would go up against former professional athletes in a series of physical events? Joe Public would get a slight head start, or advantage, and then the chase was on.

Referee John Anderson was there to ensure fair play and would start every event with the following statement:

> *"Contenders, you will go on my first whistle.*
> *Gladiators, you will go on my second whistle.*
> *Contenders, ready? Gladiators, ready?*
> *3...2...1...Pweep!"*

And if you were Adrian from Basingstoke and that whistle went, what did you do? You ran like your life depended on it.

You didn't stop and think about it. Three, two, one and you're off – 100mph, grabbing at swinging rings, bashing Wolf over the head with a pugil stick and running up an escalator the wrong way.

So the next time you get the spark of an idea you know you need to take action on – speaking up in a meeting, sending in your pitch, applying for that job, asking that person out, going down that death slide – picture John Anderson, fully decked out in his referee's outfit, whistle in mouth.

Contenders, ready?

Gladiators, ready?

3... 2... 1...

6. I LOVE IT WHEN A PLAN COMES TOGETHER

By now, you're probably thinking: "This all sounds great in theory, but how the hell does it work in the real world?"

Well, allow me to demonstrate with one particular, very big and very scary goal that I'm working on right now.

And I mean right now.

A vision of the future

Where do I get my big, scary goals from? How do I decide which goals to go after and which to leave well alone?

Once a year, usually in October (routine fans take note; same time every year), I'll sit down at my desk, turn off all interruptions, and attempt to answer the following question: "How would I like my life to be different in 12 months?"

Specifically, what do I want to:

- Start doing?
- Stop doing?
- Keep doing?
- Do more of?
- Do less of?
- Try something new?

Are there places I want to go that I haven't been to before? Are there hobbies I'd like to take up or get better at? Are there financial or business goals that I'd like to achieve or take to the next level? How do I want to spend my days? What fun stuff could I be doing this time next year that I'm not currently doing?

What I'm looking to do here is create a gap – a level of disconnect between where I am now and where I want to be in a year's time. Not that I'm unhappy with where I am right now, not at all. But I will be unhappy if I haven't made some worthy progress towards some ambitious goals after a year's hard graft.

Growth is one of my key drivers, so imagining that a year has passed and I've stayed still is painful to me. I'm looking to use that pain to create a gap.

Now < 12 months' time.

Once I've got my list of what's contained in that gap, I'll head to Google images and find relevant pictures that stand out and are memorable to me. I'll choose one picture for each goal I want to achieve in the next year and then drop all those images into an online collage maker (I use PicMonkey, but others are available), and create a vision board.

This vision board then acts as a reminder of your goals. Put it somewhere you'll see it every day, so it can enter your subconscious. I've got mine set as my desktop background on my laptop, so I see it every time I fire up my computer.

Some of our One Percenters have set it as the screensaver on their phone or just printed off and pinned above their desk. You could even get it made into a large canvas print and hang it in your living room if you want.

The key thing about the images on my vision board is that they represent the gap between where I am at the start of each year and where I want to be by the end.

Some of the goals on mine included:

- Valuing my time above ALL else – including money.
- Only doing work that I love and nothing else.
- Changing my property investments and sports betting business to run hands-free.
- Helping Jack pass the 11+ exam and get into his dream school.
- Booking an Italian cruise.
- Getting and training a new puppy.
- Hitting my health goals (which I've carried forward from previous years).
- Giving boxing a try (this will help the above goal!).
- Getting and improving upon a golf handicap.
- Focusing on angel investment.
- Booking a ski holiday.
- Seeing some of my favourite bands.
- Making the most of my "get rich slowly" funds.
- Writing my second book – Routine Machine.

That last one sounds familiar and, of course, that's the project I'm working on right now. Literally, as we speak.

So, taking that as just one of many big, scary goals that I've set myself for the next year (I'll let you decide whether or not that's scarier than being punched in the face), how do I decide what to tackle first?

The problem with to-do lists

Most people are familiar with the concept of a to-do list. That massive list of all the stuff you'd love to get done today or this week or this month. It's a magical list that never seems to get any smaller, no matter how many tasks you manage to tick off.

You start the day with 13 items on your to-do list, but by lunchtime you've added another five or six. You slog your guts out all day long and glance at your to-do list before you go and – 14 items!

Argh!

You've worked your arse off and somehow ended the day with more to do than when you started.

Then you start thinking about tomorrow. You've got that phone call with the new client, and the meeting with HR, and those reports to finish, and... oh, what's this? An email from your boss.

Now tomorrow's to-do list has 23 things on it, already.

But that's not the biggest problem with to-do lists, oh no! The main reason I hate to-do lists is our natural tendency to do the easy stuff first.

We glance down that mammoth list of 23 items and our thought process isn't which would give you the greatest return on investment or have the biggest impact on your goals.

No, we think more along the lines of, "Blimey, 23 items. Give me some quick wins so I can get this list under 15, ASAP."

Our single focus is on reducing the *number* of things left to do. We do not care that the items left are the really hard (and probably more important) tasks that we've been putting off for weeks or months. We don't care that these items are the ones that will actually move the needle for us. No, as long as the to-do list gets shorter, that's the important thing.

You'll get to the important stuff eventually, of course, because we try to do everything on our to-do list. That's why it's called a "to-do" list – it's *all* the things you *have* to do.

I don't use to-do lists.

I use *could-do* lists.

This is the antithesis to the bog-standard to-do list. It's effectively a brain dump of everything you could do to grow the business. I like to complete a full brain dump every 90 days and will usually end up with a could-do list that's several pages long and has 100 or more items on it.

There'll be lots of big scary things on there, as well as some stuff that is really speculative and may not be worthwhile pursuing. But that's fine, because I'm not actually committing to doing anything on this list.

It's a *could*-do list, not a *should*-do list.

When the time comes to choose what to do, I don't do the first thing that pops into my brain or tackle the first email in my inbox. I consult my could-do list and work out what will give me the best return on investment.

You can add to your could-do list at any time. And you should. Your could-do list should be your filter for new ideas. Add all new ideas to the could-do list and if they're good enough, the cream will rise to the top and get implemented. If not, they'll fall by the wayside and you won't waste a minute pursuing them.

The magic behind this is that it stops you having an idea and then devoting a stupid amount of time to what could be a damp squib, all the while taking you away from what you *should* be doing. Anyone who's ever suffered from Shiny New Object Syndrome will know all about this.

It also ensures that no idea gets forgotten. As soon as one enters your brain, pop it on the could-do list and get back to what you *should* be doing. It'll be there waiting for you when you next come to effectively plan your time.

Speaking of which...

The next 90 days

I love working in 90-day chunks. It's a long enough period of time for you to make some serious progress towards your goals without being so far in the distance that it creates a level of disconnect where your goals seem too big and unassailable.

I've been working in this way since March 2015. I know that, because I have kept every single 90-day plan since that date which shows me not only what I've been working on, but what I've actually achieved over that time.

So, how do 90-day plans work?

To start with, you'll choose three BIG goals for the next 90-day period. To choose these three, take a look at your could-do list and pick the three things that are going to make the biggest impact on your business (or life) to get it where you want to be.

These are the three "lead dominoes" that when knocked over would cause a chain reaction, sparking huge momentum and creating the kind of domino-knocking-over spree not seen since a Domino Rally advert.

Then write down a further three mini-goals for each month. These could be smaller tasks from your could-do list or they could be the stepping stones that will actually move you towards the big three for the quarter.

If "publishing a book" is one of your big three, then you could add "write 40,000 words" as one of your mini-goals for month one, "get the book proofread and edited" as one of month two's mini-goals, and month three could see "plan book launch" as one of its three tasks.

Three big things per quarter – the massive stuff that moves you forward.

Three mini-goals per month that are either stepping stones to help you achieve your big three or smaller goals from your could-do list that are also going to move the needle in the right direction.

Overall, nine things in three months that will result in your business and life being in a much better place 90 days from now.

Week after week, day after day

It's all well and good having these lofty, big goals but the only way you'll achieve them is by doing the right stuff on a *daily* basis. By not letting life or other people's agendas get in the way of *your* goals.

A common theme among those who successfully implement routine into their daily lives is that they don't just do the right things once. They do the right things day in, day out, week after week, for months on end. Consistently.

They're not doing anything super-human or anything that you or I couldn't also do. They're simply making the right choices and taking the right actions consistently and habitually. Routinely.

I never used to be consistent enough. I'd land at my desk at 9am on a Monday morning and just react to stuff. I'd start my week stuck in my inbox, seeing what stuff I "had to deal with", rather than choosing what to work on to grow the business. Some weeks I'd smash it out of the park and create amazing sales campaigns that brought in huge piles of cash.

But on others, I'd achieve the square root of bugger all and spend the whole time chasing my tail. I'd clock off on Friday afternoon feeling completely drained of energy, having spent the entire week firefighting problems and reacting to other people's emergencies (which weren't actually emergencies), only to find that I'd forgotten to grow my business during the week.

Just about everyone can quote Michael Gerber's line from *'The E-Myth'* about "working *on* the business, not *in* the business," but how many of us actually practice what we preach and block time out every day of every week just to work *on* the business?

If you want different results, you need different routines.

So I created a weekly planner too, which is one of the simplest documents known to man.

Grab another sheet of A4 and divide it into five columns. Label these columns Monday to Friday (or whatever your working week looks like). Above those columns are two boxes. One box is labelled "This week's one thing" and the other has the title "Anything else?"

Every week you'll choose one thing that's *the* most important task of the week. It's the one that keeps you on track for your three monthly mini-goals and/or your big three for the quarter.

Write this in the "This week's one thing" box.

If you achieve nothing else except this one thing, then congratulations – you've beaten the week. You've achieved more than most people do when given the same number of days and hours.

Sure, others may get to inbox zero, they may have a smaller in-tray, and they may even be working harder while wearing their "I ♥ Hustle" badge with pride.

But they won't have actually achieved anything of merit and 90 days from now they'll still be "hustling" and "getting shit done", but their business and lifestyle will be exactly where it is now –

with them still in the hamster wheel, spinning furiously and wondering why they're not actually getting anywhere.

What else do you want to achieve this week? Are there some things that you truly have to do? These are the items to pop in the "Anything Else?" box. This is almost your could-do list for the week. But your one thing is what really matters. Once you've achieved that, then you can move onto this other stuff.

And that's exactly how you should treat it. It is "other stuff". You don't do "other stuff" until you've done the important stuff. Your one thing is working *on* your business. Anything else is working *in* your business.

So, now the week is planned out, it's time to start planning your days. I like to plan the week ahead so I'll usually complete my planner for the following week on a Friday afternoon, as one of my final tasks for the week we're in. This week ain't over till next week is planned!

I'll consult my could-do list, check my 90-day plan, decide which of my stepping stones I'm going to progress next week and choose my one thing based on that. I'll plot out anything else that I need to do and then start to put the "immovable objects" in place for the week.

The irresistible force meets the immovable object

When I was a kid, I used to love watching WWE wrestling (or WWF as it was back then). Ultimate Warrior, Macho Man Randy Savage, The Undertaker, Hacksaw Jim Duggan and Stone Cold Steve Austin were all legends in my mind. Way back in 1987, there was a match at Wrestlemania III between Hulk Hogan and André the Giant.

André René Roussimoff was literally a giant of a man. He was seven feet and four inches tall, and 525lbs of pure muscle. No opponent had ever managed to lift André off the ground.

Terry Gene Bollea, better known as Hulk Hogan, was the poster child of WWE at the time. The all-American hero, who had been world champion for three years. He had the momentum and the entire 93,000-strong crowd on his side.

Match commentator Gorilla Monsoon famously called the match the "irresistible force meets the immovable object".

When planning out your week, your "immovable objects" should be just as immovable as a 7ft 4ins, 525lbs giant of a man.

What sort of things class as an immovable object? Anything that is important enough to go in the diary a week in advance and not be moved under any circumstances.

Your one thing is an immovable object. It's *the* immovable object. Block out time every single day for a daily one thing - something that will help you achieve your monthly or big three goals - and then protect this time with your life.

Do not check your emails until you've done your one thing. No looking at videos of kittens on Facebook until you've done your hour of writing. Put your phone on silent so you can write that sales letter. Put a "do not disturb" sign on your door until that pitch is perfected. Do something every day that actually matters.

Everything else is just noise.

Once you've got your immovable objects in place, you can start to fill your days with the "other stuff". But ensure that it's done this way round. If you start with the "other stuff" first, there won't be any room for the immovable objects.

And in case you're wondering, Hulk Hogan got his immovable object out of the way by scooping up all 7ft 4ins and 525lbs of André the Giant and body-slamming him before delivering his patented leg-drop finisher and pinning the big man to retain his world heavyweight championship belt. Job done. Your turn!

Jar / Spoon, Spoon / Jar (but with rocks)

There's a famous story about a philosophy lecturer and a jar. He held aloft the jar, which was full to the brim with small rocks. "Is this jar full?" he asked the students. They all agreed that it was.

The lecturer unscrewed the lid and added some smaller pebbles, which fell between the rocks. "How about now?" he asked. Once again, the students collectively nodded their heads in agreement that the jar was now full.

So the lecturer loosened the lid once more and poured sand into the jar, giving it a good shake to ensure all the gaps between the rocks and pebbles were completely full with tiny grains of sand. "Now, at last, the jar is full," the lecturer announced. "Isn't it?"

"Of course," the students replied. "There's no room for anything else at all."

At which point the lecturer took a sip from his water bottle, unscrewed the lid of the jar once again and poured the contents of his bottle of Evian into the jar.

The philosophy lesson he was teaching was about the importance of putting those immovable objects (the rocks) into your life (the jar) first, before you add anything else (the pebbles), your everyday tasks (sand) or all the other crap that life throws at you (the water).

If you fill the jar with water and sand, there's no room for the pebbles or rocks. You have to put the immovable objects in place first. Then the other stuff fits in around it.

So let's plan out next week.

Look at your could-do list and consult your 90-day plan. Which of your big three (or stepping stones) are you going to be working towards next week?

What's the one thing that you can do next week to move you towards that goal? Write this in your "This week's one thing" box on your planner.

What else do you want to achieve next week? And what else do you *have* to do next week? Write these in the "Anything else?" box.

Block out time for any immovable objects in the relevant days. If you've got a meeting on Wednesday lunchtime, block out that space on your planner. If you want to work on your one thing first thing every morning, block that time out. Want to take Friday off to play golf? Block it out.

Once all your immovable objects are in place, you'll have a visual representation of the time available to you next week. Your very own jar with nothing but rocks in.

Your weekly plan is now complete.

Right now you're probably thinking, "But I've got all these gaps and I haven't planned out when I'm going to do all the other stuff. I've got a business to run too, you know!"

You are going to fill those gaps, don't you worry, but one day at a time.

Start with Monday. Look at the gaps available around your immovable objects. Add a pebble or two (things from the "Anything else?" box) if they will fit. Allow some time for some sand (emails, admin, etc.) if there's room for it, too.

If there isn't room for sand, there isn't room. Don't schedule it in and don't work on it. Accept that you'll either need to fit it in somewhere else in the week or that it will build and build until the sand becomes a pebble.

I'll often go days without checking email, doing paperwork or admin and then later in the week need to block out a couple of hours for "stuff". Right now, I'm focused on writing this book, so nothing else is getting into my jar. I've got my "write the book" rocks in there and nothing else.

That means that next week I may well need to block out a half day or so just to catch up with the chaos that I've created this week by ignoring all those pebbles, sand and water.

An important distinction: Don't plan Tuesday until Monday's done. The only things you *should* plan days in advance are your immovable objects – your rocks.

Fitting in the pebbles, sand and water for Tuesday should be done last thing on Monday. That way you know the state of play – how much you've got done and what you've got left to do. And you can get started immediately on Tuesday morning; hitting the ground running the minute you land at your desk rather than wasting your most productive time of the day working out what you're going to do.

Wednesday gets planned last thing on Tuesday, Thursday's schedule is designed on Wednesday night, you look at Friday's plan on Thursday night, and you end the working week on Friday by working out your one thing for next week, putting your immovable objects in place and plotting how Monday looks.

Then clock off and enjoy the weekend.

Monday morning comes and you sprint out of the blocks because you know exactly what to work on. You know what you're working towards. You know when you're working *on* the business and when you're working *in* the business. Your weekly routine is all planned out in front of you.

Let me make it easy for you

I'm a sucker for the stationery aisles at those big supermarkets – the kind where you can spend half a day browsing different types of pens, notebooks and, of course, planners.

I've used several planners over the last couple of decades. Some I have spent a bloody fortune on and others have been gifted to me. But almost all of them have something in common – they never got used.

Some got picked up for a few days or weeks with the best of intentions. But most just got thumbed through before gathering dust on a shelf somewhere. Don't get me wrong; I know first-hand that using a good planner can make a hell of a difference to your business, especially over a prolonged period of several months or more. But I just couldn't find one that did what I wanted.

I've never been able to get on with online planners or apps (as Jason will attest to, having attempted to convert me to one or another over the years). Time and time again I revert to my own, crudely-made, hand-designed planners that do *exactly* what I want them to do, which is to get me in the routine of doing the right things on a daily basis.

If you want better results, you need better routines, right?

I wanted a planner that would hold me accountable to the big plans I'd made, to achieve great things over a prolonged period of time, and to never feel overwhelmed because I'll always know what the one most important thing is that I need to do next to get me where I want to go.

Most planners are far too complex. They're designed for people who might want to plan out their day hour-by-hour from 4am all the way up to midnight (which means if you work nights, or like me do most of your productive work in a short four to six-hour period, you'll find half of the space on each page is wasted).

Then there's the padding. "I know," some bright spark said. "Let's add some motivational quotes to each page. That'll get them fired up and ready to take on the world." Erm, yeah, or another way of looking at it is you're taking up valuable world domination planning space with trite clichés that mean bugger all to anyone.

And, finally, there are the planners that need a 26-page instruction manual to be able to use them.

The planner that works best is the planner you use. And I've been using these planning tools for the last five years. That routine stuck because it was simple, not because it was clever.

You can create your own planners using sheets of A4 and a couple of tables knocked up in a word processor. I did exactly that for a couple of years and it served me well.

But when I launched the One Percent Club back in 2016, I wanted to be able to share these tools with our One Percenters. And showing them my crude attempts at functional design wasn't going to cut it. I could happily work from scraps of paper, but I needed a nice system that others could "swipe and deploy" easily.

So I got on the phone to Lee, our designer, and asked him to put together a proper, old-school planner that contained all the tools that I've used over the years to massively grow my businesses.

I designed the planner to be really simple. So simple that even I could use it because it was the planner I'd been using for the last five years. Now it's just a better designed, pretty-looking, better organised, nicely bound and professionally printed version. As opposed to the "designed by a monkey (me), created in Word, and printed at home" version that I'd been using previously.

I call it My World Domination Planner and send one to all our One Percenters every year. I love to see them a few months later, dog-eared and covered in notes and scribbles (the planners that is, not the One Percenters!).

Because the best planner in the world is the one that you use and that you're still using three months later, nine months later or five years later.

You will find details of how you can download a copy of my planner in the resources section at the end of the book.

There's a lot to take in this chapter, so let's quickly go through it all one more time:

- Start with an **annual vision board.** What do you want to change in the next 12 months?
- Build your **could-do list.** What *could* you do to make those visions a reality?
- Set your **big three goals** every 90 days.
- Work out your **monthly stepping stones** to the big three.
- Choose a **weekly one thing** to achieve the stepping stones.
- Choose a **daily one thing** to achieve the weekly one thing.
- **Write it all down.** Rocks first, then pebbles. Only add sand and water if there's space.
- **Do the work.** Build the routine. Day after day. Week after week.

Homework

Task: Take some time here to pause and reflect on your gap. What's the difference between where you are now and where you want to be in 12 months? Write down all the things you'd like to change, in every aspect of your life. Create your vision board and place it somewhere prominent.

Question: Is your jar currently full of rocks or over-spilling with sand and water?

7. LEFT FOOT, RIGHT FOOT. REPEAT IF NECESSARY.

Back when Britain actually had an empire to rule over, British soldiers used to be posted to Far Eastern outposts that were under the sovereign's rule. While away from Blighty, they used to try to catch the local wild monkeys to keep as pets.

Despite being the King's best soldiers, they couldn't outsmart and capture these wild creatures. The men might have been stronger, more intelligent, able to work as a team, and armed to the teeth, but they were still never able to outwit the monkeys.

Then the natives showed them how it could be done.

In a clearing in the jungle, they placed a cage with large items of fruit at the bottom – the perfect bait for a peckish primate. The cage had a narrow opening at the top, just large enough for the monkey to squeeze its arm through.

Then the humans waited. And waited.

Eventually, a curious monkey would investigate the cage. It could see and smell the fruit inside, but how to reach it? After some time, it would find the narrow opening at the top of the cage, slide its arm in and grab the fruit.

It would then attempt to retract its arm from the cage, only to find that it now wouldn't fit through the opening because it was holding on to the pieces of fruit. It wasn't about to let go of this prize find though; it's not every day you see quality fruit like this laying around for a monkey to help himself to.

So the monkey remains trapped of its own free will. All he has to do to escape is let go of the fruit, but he doesn't. He stays trapped, refusing to give up his spoils.

At this point, the natives very slowed crept up on the monkey, encircling him, but being very careful not to startle him or attract his attention in any way. He was focused on the fruit in his hand and they wanted it to stay that way.

Eventually, the humans could get within grabbing distance of the monkey and were able to capture him with very little effort.

They used no weapons. They didn't use their brute force. They weren't faster than the monkey. They didn't simply out-number or out-work him.

They used patience. A slow approach, waiting for the monkey to do all the work and slowly, one step at a time, crept up on the unsuspecting primate and nabbed him for the Brits.

Or, as they explained to the soldiers in broken English: "Slowly, slowly, catchy monkey."

It's really tempting when planning new habits and routines to do a complete 180 and do the complete opposite of what you're doing right now.

After all, if you want completely different results, you need completely different routines, right?

Of course, but you also want routines that stick. Sticky the stick insect stuck on a sticky bun, remember?

Little and often will always beat one-off binges just as waves create sand by wearing down rock one wave at a time, hundreds of times a day, every day, for hundreds of thousands of years.

The water is but a tiny snowflake. But it has a nice long hill of time and it's been rolling its snowball down the hill for millennia now. A tsunami alone can't turn rocks into sand. The drip, drip, drip of slow, methodical routine over the long term is far more powerful.

Think about how your hair grows or your nails or skin. Constantly, a tiny amount at a time; so small and inconsequentially that you wouldn't even notice the difference from one day to the next or even one week to the next. Yet go a few months without cutting your hair or nails and see what a huge difference the drip, drip, drip makes.

A dripping tap appears to waste very little water. Just one tiny droplet at a time, every ten seconds or so. But the dripping tap is relentless. It never misses a beat.

If that dripping tap had green sticky dots to chart its progress, it would have an unbroken streak of 100,000 drips in no time at all. Every ten seconds, regular as clockwork – drip. Six times a minute – drip. Every minute of every hour. Every hour of every day. That's 60,480 drips in one week, with not a single drip being missed.

Put the plug in the sink and after an hour or so you'll see the cumulative effect of those tiny drips. Go on holiday for a fortnight and you'd be coming home to a very wet floor.

This is what routine looks like. It's a drop in the ocean in the short term. In the long term, it creates oceans.

Get rich slowly

When I launched my internet marketing company in 2000, there were just three things that could possibly have stopped me:

1. I knew nothing about marketing.
2. I'd never run a company before.
3. I didn't own a computer, let alone have access to the internet.

I bought a copy of *'Internet Marketing for Dummies'*. That took care of #1.

I spoke with an accountant, who told me what I needed to do to run a company. That's #2 checked.

Finally, to solve #3, I borrowed my girlfriend's parents' computer, which had access to the internet. It was slow-as-treacle 56k dialup, but it was a whole new world for me. I'd gone from zero to one.

The very first thing I did when I got online was to search Alta Vista (yep, that was the Google of the time!) for the phrase "make money online". I didn't want to check the weather, join a chatroom or any of the other things that people were getting online for.

No, I wanted to earn some money. I was stuck in a day job I hated and this was going to be my way out. I'd heard about all these dotcom millionaires, getting paid millions upon millions simply for having an idea for a website. They didn't even need to make a profit. I could do that!

How hard can it be to run a company at a loss? As long as it's a "good idea", I'll be a millionaire this time next year. Hence, the guy that knows nothing about marketing, nothing about running a company, and doesn't own a computer launches an internet marketing company.

And what does that company *do*? Well, it teaches other people how to make money on the internet, of course. That thing I don't know how to do myself.

My internet marketing business has evolved quite a bit from those early days of pushing "get paid to surf", "get paid to read emails" and "get paid to click on stuff" MLM programmes, but that mindset I had two decades ago still exists in others today.

At a Berkshire Hathaway AGM, Charlie Munger was asked by a young shareholder how he might follow in Munger and Buffett's footsteps. Charlie's reply was as cutting as it was insightful:

"We get these questions a lot from the enterprising young. You look at some old guy who's rich and you ask 'How can I become like you... only faster?'

Spend each day trying to be a little wiser than you were when you woke up. Discharge your duties faithfully and well. Step by step you get ahead, but not necessarily in fast spurts. Slug it out one inch at a time, day by day.

At the end of the day – if you live long enough – most people get what they deserve."

In the UK, approximately 14,800 people searched Google for the term "make money online" last month. I wonder how many of them will stick at "slugging it out one inch at a time" and whether they'll "get what they deserve" 20 years from now?

A further 5,400 people were a little less patient, searching for "make money fast". One can only assume that some of those people are now missing a kidney or two.

Get rich quick schemes have been derided since the day dot and yet we still want results *now*. We don't want to wait. We don't want to be patient. We don't want to bother with the slowly, slowly. Just give us the damn monkey already.

We want our favourite box sets available on demand for us to binge-watch an entire series. We expect next day delivery as standard, even on a Sunday. We want our burger and fries freshly cooked, but ready in 90 seconds. We want to be famous and we want to be rich.

Freddie Mercury summed it up: "I want it all, I want it all, I want it all, and I want it now!"

How many people do you think googled the term "get rich slowly" last month? The answer is ten.

Ten people. You could count them on your fingers and toes without needing to take your socks off.

You see, getting rich slowly isn't sexy or cool. It won't get you on the cover of Heat magazine next month. But it will make you rich.

The main difference between getting rich quickly and getting rich slowly is the success rate. Very few people who take the "get rich quick" path will actually achieve significant wealth. And those that do are infinitely more likely to lose the lot again.

In 2005, Pete Kyle won £5.1million on the UK National Lottery. Three years later, he'd blown the lot and was living on benefits, last seen living at a £15-a-night hostel sandwiched between a sex shop and a tattoo parlour.

Pete's story isn't a solitary tale. Unbelievably, 70 per cent of lottery winners go broke and a third of them end up declaring bankruptcy. Who'd have thought that by suddenly getting a cheque for a few million quid, you'd go from a 0.16 per cent chance of bankruptcy to a 33.33 per cent chance?

Meanwhile, those ten people that look for ways to "get rich slowly" start laying down some solid foundations.

They set up an ISA and a pension. They start "pound cost averaging" into those accounts. They live within their means. They learn how to invest in the stock market or property or art. They learn how businesses work and continually work on their own personal development. They develop the skill to be able to manage money so that when they do have an abundance of it, they won't squander it like a lottery winner.

They build, buy, acquire and sweat assets. Those assets throw off excess cash which they can use to buy more assets.

If the "get rich quick" brigade somehow suddenly found themselves with a big pile of money, they'd buy liabilities with it, which as Rich Dad 101 will tell you, takes money out of your pocket until that new-found wealth is all gone.

It's the tortoise and the hare all over again, and we all know how that race ended.

Fancy owning… the world? [*Cue evil laugh*]

The average British adult retires with savings of around £30,000. To maintain their current standard of living, they would actually need a pension pot containing more than £675,000. So why is there a gap of £645,000 and what can we do to fill it?

There are several reasons why there's such a chasm between what people need to save and what they actually do save:

1. The Baby Boomer generation retired with good pensions. Final salary schemes. Jobs for life with a company that guaranteed a good pension as part of the package. A state pension that could be drawn at 65 (or 60 for women) with plenty more workers paying into the pot (still working) than drawing out (retired). That's the model we see, so we assume it'll be the same for us. It won't.
2. The "pain" of living in poverty throughout your retirement is decades away. Whereas the pain of going without that £70 a month now will be felt right now. People would rather have a feast today and worry about putting food on the table in a few decades time.
3. Investing seems hard. It's something that's best left to the bankers. And look what a mess they made of it in 2008.
4. It seems pointless. If you're earning the UK average salary of £27,000 per year, building up a pension pot of £675,000 seems completely pie-in-the-sky.

The best person I know to dispel these myths is Andrew Craig. In his excellent book *'How to Own the World: A Plain English Guide to Thinking Globally and Investing Wisely'*, Andrew assures readers that if you can learn how to drive a car then you can learn to look after your money.

He demonstrates how making money through investments is far easier than you've always thought and that you can achieve much more than you first believed possible – especially if you have the "hill of time" on your side.

There is no better expert to manage your finances, Andrew declares, than yourself. You now have access to more markets, more reports and more information than the world's best hedge fund managers did 20 years ago. Those tools are more powerful and cheaper than they have ever been.

Andrew's underlying message is to take control of your own investments. That doesn't mean you need to start picking individual stocks or checking the price of oil every five minutes.

Andrew's key to long-term investment success is to "own the world".

Buy everything – tech stocks, oil and mining sectors, real estate, precious metals, pharmaceutical companies and media giants. Buy into the US, Europe, Asia, the Far East, you name it.

The world economy keeps on growing. As long as you own a slice of everything, it's a rising tide that will lift all ships. Sure, some sectors will soar and others will tank. When one country has a boom, there'll be another with a bust.

But owning the world takes the guesswork out of it. You don't need to pick the winners and avoid the losers. You own a slice of everything.

You no longer need to care whether the markets go up or down. If they go up, you've made more money. If they go down, your next purchase of "the world" is at a discount. You use the drip, drip, drip routine of pound cost averaging to smooth out the peaks and troughs of the market.

Don't worry, you don't need to physically go out and buy shares in every company on the entire planet. There are funds in which you can invest to track certain sectors or certain territories.

Andrew has his own fund, which is available to invest in through a standard stocks and shares ISA that replicates his "own the world" strategy.

But, as Andrew goes to great lengths to re-enforce, you are perfectly capable of learning to do this yourself. A little education, some automatic systems and maybe an hour of your time once a year to rebalance your portfolio (ensuring that you're still "owning the world" rather than going in too heavy in one sector or region) and you've just taken care of your financial future.

You can start to chip away at that £645,000 gap and ensure that you're not relying on the 40/40/40 retirement plan like the rest of the country where you spend 40 years working 40 hours a week to then retire and try to live on 40 per cent of your salary.

How do you eat an elephant?

Having set these massive goals, how do you set about getting started? How do we make the big, scary goals more palatable?

Exactly the same way you'd eat an elephant – one bite at a time.

Take a minute now to think very hard about exactly where you want to be 12 months or even 90 days from now, whether that's in terms of website traffic levels, revenue, membership numbers, etc. What needs to happen to achieve those targets?

How much content needs to be written? How many emails need to be sent? How many sales campaigns need to be launched? How much advertising needs to be done?

If at this point you've not given up at the prospect of all that work, then congratulations (either that or you've grossly underestimated the work you need to do). Now you need to plan how you're going to do all that work. Most people would rush in, trying to do as much of it as possible and a week or two later, when they're not rolling in money, they give up.

It's far better to take the "eat an elephant" approach. In much the same way as pound cost averaging makes investing in the stock market a smoother ride, doing very little every day on a regular basis will, over a long period of time, result in greater success than rushing in all guns blazing.

Back in the day (aka a long time ago) I used to run an affiliate marketing blog. Here's a blog post I wrote about eating elephants:

> *"I've been following a simple formula every day since April: A little PPC ("pay per click" marketing – think Google Ads), a little SEO (search engine optimisation), and a little networking every day. Nearly six months later and I'm only just really starting to see the results of swapping from my previous routine of just trying to get everything done as quickly as possible.*
>
> *The difference is astonishing. Whereas I'd previously had trouble getting motivated in the mornings (mainly due to not knowing where to start), I'm now straight into the swing of things. And whereas I'd be burned out by Wednesday every week and still working through every weekend, I'm now finding that my much smaller to-do list is getting cleared by mid-afternoon most days, leaving me free to go out*

walking with the dogs, ride my bike or just play some Wii or PS2.

Even more astonishingly is that doing less every day has resulted in my affiliate earnings going up. We're now making £9,000 a month more profit than in April – and it's not really that surprising when you think why that is. Every single day for the last six months I've done something towards the important stuff: Google loves regularly updated sites and most of ours have been updated every day pretty much without fail, we've got hundreds more inbound links, we've managed to put up around 400 PPC campaigns, and we've made loads of great contacts and new partnerships.

Of course, life will throw things at you to put you off course, you'll have emergencies to deal with, priorities will change, and you'll have days where you just can't get motivated. In which case, give yourself the day off – or the week if you like. Then get back in the regular habit of a bit of PPC, a bit of SEO and a bit of networking.

Don't set your targets too high: I work full time at affiliate marketing and aim to do three PPC campaigns a day, an hour of content and around an hour networking (which normally means playing on Facebook, posting on affiliate forums or chatting to people on Messenger). It gives me enough "spare time" to ensure that I can deal with anything else that might need doing or just head off to the driving range at 2pm knowing I've already done a full day's work and I'm still raring to go come Friday afternoon (although the pub is still calling by then).

What if you're still working the day job or at uni, etc.? Well, you should be able to spare an hour a day (I used to work on my affiliate business 9am to 12pm, then my full-time job from 1pm to 9pm, and still do a few hours in the evening on affiliate marketing), so aim to do one PPC campaign a day, 20 minutes SEO work and ten minutes networking. Now that might not sound like a lot, but give it six months and you'll have done approximately 130 PPC campaigns, 43 hours of SEO work and 21 hours of networking. That should put you well on the way to giving up the day job if you wish.

You will need a degree of patience, as this approach brings steady results rather than instant ones. Most people would give up if they don't see big bucks within a month or two, but you should be prepared to give it at least four months before seeing any impact on your cashflow (as I've said, I'm only just starting to see a major impact after six months). Just don't give up. You've only got to do a little bit each day and that's not so hard, is it?

There's no doubt at all that I'm going to continue with this "eat an elephant" approach to my business and there's no reason why it can't transfer into any part of your life. Want to lose weight? Don't bother joining a gym, working yourself into the ground for two weeks and then giving up like most people do. Just do a little more exercise every day (walk to the shops and get a paper?) and eat a little less crap.

Speaking of eating, I'd better sign off. My elephant's going cold."

Reading my own words back several years later, I'm struck by a couple of thoughts. Firstly, this blog post was written around the time I was discovering that I could achieve more by working fewer hours.

It's interesting to see in black and white how I was feeling at the time – struggling to get motivated in the mornings (I wasn't sleeping anywhere near enough), burned out by Wednesday lunchtime every week (working 16+ hour days will do that to you), and working through just about every single weekend (trying to clear that never-ending to-do list).

It's also abundantly clear to me that this blog was written pre-kids. There's talk of playing computer games, long walks with the dogs and spending my new-found free time at the driving range or at a place you'd never find me these days – the pub.

Why was I suddenly able to earn more money by doing less? Because I'd triaged what I was doing and ensured I was working every day on the three most important tasks that would grow my revenues – advertising, marketing and networking.

In those three areas, I broke the big, scary targets down into daily, manageable, bite-size chunks. I made a new target and one that I could achieve every single day.

Anytime you find yourself feeling overwhelmed, make those slices of elephant more, well, bite-sized. Break that big, scary goal up into smaller chunks and then work consistently, habitually, *routinely* on those chunks.

Take one baby step and then another, safe in the knowledge that every single tiny step you take will move you closer to actually achieving that massive, scary goal. If you keep putting one foot in front of the other, you *will* get there.

It's not about the bike

British Cycling used to be a bit of a joke. We Brits would be bringing up the rear, huffing and puffing our way up the mountain well behind the leaders. Hopes of Olympic glory and Tour de France wins were but a dream.

Enter Sir Dave Brailsford. Sir Dave joined the British Cycling team in 1997 and became performance director in 2003. The following year, Team GB won four medals at the Olympics in Athens, including golds for now-Sirs Bradley Wiggins and Chris Hoy. It was the team's best performance in 96 years. And four years later, at the 2008 games in Beijing, they would pick up a record 14 medals, including eight golds.

Having seen what Sir Dave's methods had done for Team GB, he was persuaded to join Team Sky to head up their road cycling team with a view to replicating his success on the grandest cycling stage of them all – the Tour de France. It was a race that no Brit had ever won and one which is widely accepted as the world's toughest bike race.

Riders compete over a three-week period, covering more than 3,500 kilometres of gruelling climbs, with competitors often having to ascend multiple mountains in a single day from altitudes of a few hundred feet above sea level to more than 3,000ft – all while racing against their fiercest competitors and in 30c-degree heat.

It took Sir Dave just two years to work his magic, with Bradley Wiggins becoming the first Brit to win the Tour de France in 2012. The same year saw another 12 cycling medals picked up by Team GB at the London Olympics, including another gold for Wiggins, who got his knighthood as a result.

As if to prove that it was no fluke, Team Sky won the race again in 2013, this time with Chris Froome wearing the yellow jersey.

Froome would go onto notch up four TdF victories, including three in a row from 2015 to 2017 – the first rider to do so since Lance Armstrong, who of course had his own "methods" to give him an edge over his rivals.

As I write this, Team Sky have won six of the last seven Tour de France competitions and Team GB have notched up 42 Olympic cycling medals in the last four games, including 24 golds.

Not bad for a laughing stock.

So what was the secret to Dave Brailsford's success? Did he have a golden generation of athletes, all perfectly suited to be the best in the world at cycling? Did he stumble across a new bike that went faster than everyone else's? Nope. In Sir Dave's own words, "It's not about the bike."

What Brailsford did have was a technique that he referred to as the "aggregation of marginal gains". What the hell does that mean? Well, it may sound complicated, but it's actually a pretty simple idea.

While everyone else is focused on getting world class at a small number of things (like building bigger muscles, improving stamina and making the bikes more efficient and reliable), Dave and his team would break down the big, unachievable goal (winning the Tour de France or an Olympic gold medal) into each individual element that could help or hinder them.

They'd then look to improve each of those elements by just one per cent. As Brailsford said in 2012: "The whole principle came from the idea that if you broke down everything you could think of that goes into riding a bike and then improved it by one per cent, you will get a significant increase when you put them all together again."

The bike went into a wind tunnel to improve aerodynamics by one per cent. He insisted everyone in the team used antibacterial hand gel to cut down illness and infections by one per cent. The team bus was redesigned to improve recuperation by one per cent. And when he discovered dust accumulating on the floor of the mechanic's truck, he had the floor painted pristine white so it would be noticed one per cent quicker.

He employed psychologists to tease out one per cent improvements in the athletes' mindset. He redesigned the team's training suits and helmets to make them one per cent more comfortable, reduce friction by one per cent, wick sweat away one per cent better, and reduce air drag by one per cent.

Sir Dave went hunting for each and every one of the team's weaknesses – those tiny opportunities that had been allowed to slide. And by correcting each one, he saw that desired one per cent improvement and went hunting for the next "marginal gain" to be had.

While on the road for the Tour de France, he noticed that the entire team, not just the athletes, were getting more and more tired as the weeks rolled on. Twenty-three nights of sleeping on different mattresses in different hotels will do that to you.

So a new bus followed the team around, containing each person's preferred mattress and pillow. It's fair to say they slept more than one per cent better as a result, and having every single member of the team firing on all cylinders throughout the gruelling three-week process cannot be underestimated.

Not just for middle-aged men in Lycra

Team GB's women's hockey team also employed marginal gains to win a gold medal. They went as far as installing an exact replica of the 2016 Olympic pitch at their training ground and practicing in intense heat during cold UK winters in order to replicate the weather they would likely compete in during a summer in Brazil.

The airline industry has been employing marginal gains for several decades, always looking for every opportunity, however small, to increase safety. When any airline discovers such an opportunity, they immediately share it with all their rival airlines and the whole industry benefits.

Imagine every airline in the world constantly looking out for ways to make one tiny item one per cent safer and then every other airline adopting it. That's why the airline industry is one of the safest in the world. In 1912, more than half of all US Army pilots died in crashes. By 2014, the average crash rate for the major airlines was one plane out of every 8.3million take-offs. That's some aggregation of marginal gains, right there!

Adding all those one per cent gains back together is where the magic really happens.

Every year in New York, the annual Nathan's Hot Dog Eating Contest takes place. The rules are simple. Competitors have 12 minutes to eat as many hot dogs as possible. Most people employ the "shove them all in my mouth and chew like mad" strategy and that has served the winners well for a long time.

Or it did until Takeru Kobayashi came along with a marginal gains strategy. He discovered that by breaking the hot dogs in half, rather than eating it whole, he left his hands free for loading the next dog and it gave him more room for chewing.

Next, he tried separating the sausage from the bread and dunking the bread in water so it dissolved easier in his mouth. He videoed his training sessions and watched them back, looking for the opportunities to find another one per cent gain. He tweaked his posture, tested the difference between standing and sitting, employed different chewing techniques and swallowed at different intervals.

Once he had the optimum setup for each element, he stitched all those marginal gains back together and headed to NYC. His competitors were all seasoned professionals, most of them weighing in at twice the size of Kobayashi. He didn't stand a chance.

Or so they thought.

Kobayashi blew them out of the water with the aggregation of his marginal gains. He blitzed through an unbelievable 50 hotdogs in 12 minutes – double the previous world record. He would go on to smash his own record three more times, as he won the competition every year for six years straight.

Kobayashi has used the same marginal gains techniques to become the world record holder for eating grilled cheese sandwiches (13 in one minute), buffalo wings (337 in 30 minutes), pizza (62 slices in 12 minutes), lamb hot pots (55 in 24 minutes) and tacos (129 in ten minutes).

And, somehow, he's still skinnier than me.

Could a one per cent change double your business?

Do you think you could use Sir Dave Brailsford's aggregation of marginal gains philosophy to effectively double the size of your business in a little over a year?

Let me ask you this. Hand on heart; do you think you could grow your business by just one per cent this week? No 10x'ing things here. Just a simple one per cent change.

And then one per cent next week? One per cent growth again the week after? Rinse and repeat. Week after week.

Do that for 69 weeks and – hey presto! – you've just doubled your business! Yep, because of the aggregation of those marginal gains, it only takes 69 one per cent tweaks to achieve 100 per cent growth.

Could you get one per cent better at selling? Increase your profit margins by one per cent? Be one per cent more focused and do one per cent more marketing? Reduce wastage by one per cent and train your staff to be one per cent more effective?

Tick off simple one per cent improvements in your finances, mindset, learning, networking, communications, copywriting, negotiation and people management?

Get one per cent more people seeing your ads? Persuade one per cent more of them to click on the ad? Get one per cent more prospects to sign up for your lead magnet and then increase your email open rates by one per cent?

Get one per cent more people buying, and spending one per cent more money on one per cent more items? Reduce your refunds or cancellations by one per cent? Get customers taking upsells one per cent more often, returning to buy again one per cent more often, and referring one per cent more of their friends?

Collect one per cent more testimonials and one per cent more reviews? Post one per cent more often on social media with offers that are one per cent better than what you're doing right now?

Do just one of those things every week, with a tiny one per cent improvement, and 69 weeks later – BOOM! – you've just doubled your business.

Unless you're already running a perfectly oiled machine with every single moving part working at 100 per cent capacity, improving a single element by just one per cent should be easily achievable for just about every single one of us.

If you can get one per cent better every day, you'll be 37 times better a year from now.

Conversely, if you got one per cent worse every day for a year, you'd be practically at zero in 12 months' time.

Stacking up these one per cent improvements is exactly what my One Percent Club is all about. (You can find details about it in the resources section at the end of the book.)

I'm just going outside, I may be some time

In 1911, a bloke from Plymouth had a bit of a lofty goal. He wanted to become the first man ever to set foot upon the southern-most part of Earth – the South Pole. That man was Captain Robert Falcon Scott.

As a child growing up in Plymouth, I remember learning about this local hero and the exhausting, never-ending trek that Scott and his team ultimately gave their lives for in the name of King and country.

Captain Scott – together with Edward Wilson, Henry Bowers, Edgar Evans and Lawrence Oates – set off from their base camp on the west side of Ross Island in Antarctica on November 1st 1911 to make the 895-mile journey to the South Pole.

Seventy-eight days later, on January 18th 1912, Scott and his team arrived at the South Pole – only to be greeted by a tent, flapping in the bitter wind.

They had been beaten to the Pole.

Inside the tent was a note. Norwegian explorer Roald Amundsen had set out on the same journey to 90 degrees south at roughly the same time as Captain Scott. But Amundsen had arrived on December 14th, 1911 – 35 days before Scott and his party.

Defeated and demoralised, Scott's party began the gruelling trek back to base camp. The weather turned extraordinarily adverse, food rations were in critically short supply and the team were slowed greatly by injuries sustained in falls, as well as the effects of scurvy and frostbite.

Edgar Evans died from a blow to the head suffered in a fall on February 17th. By mid-March, Lawrence Oates' feet had become severely frostbitten, which slowed the entire group's progress.

In order to meet the pre-laid food deposits and avoid starving, the men needed to travel nine miles per day. However, Oates' injuries had slowed them to an average of just three miles a day. On March 15th, Captain Oates walked out of the tent into a -40c blizzard, telling the remaining men: "I am just going outside, and may be some time."

Oates sacrificed himself so that Scott, Wilson and Bowers might live. The remaining three men continued for another 20 miles towards the "One Ton" food depot that would save their lives, but were stopped in their tracks by a fierce blizzard.

Trapped in their tent, too weak and too cold to continue, they died nine days later on March 29th. Their frozen bodies were recovered by a search party in November of the following year. They were just 11 miles short of the food station.

Oates's body was never found.

It says a lot about my upbringing that Scott's story stuck with me. I've always been one to champion the underdog. I support small businesses over big conglomerates. I cheer for the bad guy in movies. I follow Plymouth Argyle. How much of that comes from studying this local hero, who gave his life so valiantly but ultimately fell short?

I don't recall learning about Roald Amundson at school. Yet he was the guy who won. He was the one who defeated Captain Scott. Amundson beat him to the South Pole by more than a month and made it back safely, almost without incident.

How did Amundson make it look so easy, while Scott's team struggled and ultimately perished?

The way Amundson approached the quest was (to excuse a pun) the polar opposite of Scott's. Scott would adapt his tactics on a daily basis. When the weather turned bad, Scott would stay in his tent and make zero progress. When conditions were perfect, he would push his men ever harder, asking them to slowly inch forward for up to nine hours at a time.

After a few nine-hour days in a row, Scott's men would become demoralised and physically exhausted. He had little choice but to let them rest, so they would hole up in their tent, again making no progress.

Amundson, by comparison, kept to the same routine almost every day. His team would ski, sledge, and trek for between five and six hours, covering an average of 15 miles a day every single day, no matter what the weather.

Good conditions? Fifteen miles, then rest up. Bad conditions? Fifteen miles, then a much-needed rest. Awful conditions? Fifteen miles or as near as dammit.

Roald Amundson was a Routine Machine.

Fifteen miles a day wasn't a walk in the park. It was tough and incredibly demanding at times. But it wasn't as physically and mentally exhausting as Scott's plan. And it was more effective. Amundson won the race and Scott died.

Amundson's whole team knew what the strategy was: Put one foot in front of the other until we've walked 15 miles and then we rest. It's the same every day. And every four days, we'll be one degree of latitude closer to the Pole.

Being able to visualise constant, never-ending progress on the map every single day was incredibly motivating for the Norwegians, while Scott and his team might spend a week freezing their bits off and hardly moving at all.

Sometimes, you just need to put one foot in front of the other. Left foot, right foot. Repeat if necessary.

Homework

Question: What's your equivalent to "15 miles a day"?

Task: Think about all the one per cent improvements you could make. List them out and start stacking them up.

8. THE WRITE STUFF

Stephen King has written 59 bestselling novels and more than 200 short stories. His books have sold more than 350million copies. But Stephen King doesn't write books.

He just writes.

An average of ten pages per day, every day.

Stephen King is a Routine Machine. "If I don't write every day, the characters begin to stale off in my mind. I begin to lose my hold on the story's plot and pace," says King.

Over a three-month period, that simple "ten pages a day" routine amounts to a 180,000-word novel. King adds: "The first draft of a book – even a long one – should take no more than three months." He feels that by dragging the process out beyond three months, the story starts to feel a little foreign and the writing process starts to feel like hard work.

Once the first draft is complete, King then takes an extended break of around six weeks to rest and recuperate and allow the story to "settle". He can then revisit the draft with an open mind and fresh perspective, allowing him to spot glaring plot holes or inconsistent character traits more easily.

"When you write a book, you spend day after day scanning and identifying the trees," he says. "When you're done, you have to step back and look at the forest."

The forest isn't the only thing that Stephen King is looking at. He's primed his environment by lining up lots and lots of "monkey see, monkey do" visual clues to help make his "ten pages a day" routine easy.

He says: "I have a glass of water or a cup of tea. There's a certain time I sit down, from 8.00 to 8.30, somewhere within that half hour every morning. I have my vitamin pill and my music, sit in the same seat, and the papers are all arranged in the same places.

The cumulative purpose of doing these things the same way every day seems to be a way of saying to the mind, you're going to be dreaming soon."

And what does one of the world's most prolific writers do when he's not writing? He reads, of course! When asked on Twitter recently how many books he reads in an average year, King replied: "About 80. So many books, so little time."

In an average year, King reads more than ten million words. Ten pages a day sees him writing a further 720,000 words each and every year. And he's been doing this for the last 45 years. That's how a person who doesn't write books sells 350million of them.

Sir Terry Pratchett also wrote every single day, but whereas Stephen King would focus on one novel for three months solid and then rest and recuperate, Pratchett would just keep on writing, often having several books on the go at any one time.

At the time of his death in 2015, Sir Terry had written more than 70 books, including 41 in the Discworld series. He averaged two books per year. He also left behind as many as ten incomplete, unpublished works on his computer. The works, which were at various stages of development, were destroyed after Sir Terry's death – at his request – with his hard drive being crushed by a steamroller.

Having so many of his novels set in the same world, it was easier for Pratchett to have multiple stories at various stages of development, as characters and subplots would often cross over into other stories. He didn't tend to overthink things either, much preferring the "arse in chair, hands on keyboard" approach that I'm currently employing to deliver these words to you.

In an interview with Writing Magazine in 2012, Sir Terry said:

"Generally, I don't have a plan but I do have an instinct. You can always rewrite, check things, find the right way to say things. If you sit and plan, you get stuck in the planning. When you're writing a book, I find my fingers just start doing it. It sounds like magic."

He also didn't feel the need to write in order, often penning an individual segment for one book before hopping to a completely new scene in a totally different story. He would piece them together into something that resembled a beginning, middle and end later.

What mattered first and foremost was that he wrote. Every single day. Sir Terry Pratchett was a Routine Machine.

"Writing is my ground state of being. It's what, on the whole, I think I should be doing, so everything else that I'm doing is time filched from writing. I resent it if I can't do it. I'm not disciplined, but if left to myself, I'd do a lot of writing every day."

Both King and Pratchett had a brilliant, built-in defence against writer's block, the scourge of authors everywhere. If you're working on something and the creativity just won't come, simply work on something else. But get to work. Ten pages a day or whatever your equivalent to "15 miles a day" is.

Sir Terry said: "There's no such thing as writer's block. That was invented by people in California who couldn't write." Meanwhile, Stephen King said: "Amateurs sit and wait for inspiration, the rest of us just get up and go to work."

Comparing myself to Stephen King

It's only natural that after talking about such literary icons as Stephen King and the late, great Sir Terry Pratchett, that I should now elevate myself (in my own mind at least) to the same level and talk about *my* writing process.

Of course, Pratchett has sold a *few* more books than me and King might be a *slightly* better writer but, then again, they've had a few decades' head-start. I'm sure people will eventually look back on my works with the same high regard that *'Carrie'* or *'The Colour of Magic'* hold after all these years.

OK, maybe not.

But there's one thing you can't take away that I do have in common with the aforementioned icons – I am a published author. Not on their scale, I grant you. I'm averaging one book every two years, compared to Terry Pratchett's two per year – and even this book shouldn't have existed.

"I'm never writing another book again," remember? Those were the words I uttered at the launch party for *'Big Ideas...'* and I meant every damn word.

Writing a book is bloody hard work. It took me around four months to write my first and it wasn't a process I particularly enjoyed. Sure, I enjoy writing. But this isn't just writing. This is creating a book. A whole bloody book. That all has to make sense. And flow. And explain complex things in simple ways.

My "process" back then was to write and write and write. And after I'd done all that writing I then had to try to get it to flow in a natural way. This was when I discovered that the Chapter Three I'd written actually made more sense as Chapter 19, and that my original Chapter Ten would be the new Chapter Five. So now, all the references back to Chapter Three from Chapter Ten are now in Chapter Five and now refer back to a chapter that you haven't actually read yet.

Clear as mud, right? It was a bit like that scene in Back to the Future II, where Doc has to get a blackboard out to explain the alternate 1985, 1955 and 2015 timelines to Marty.

I didn't write *'Big Ideas...'* routinely. I'd write for a few hours when I found the time or block out a day here and there. After four long, hard months, I thought I was done.

I proudly presented my completed manuscript to my book coach and publisher, announcing that the "hard work was done" and now we *only* needed to proofread, edit, format, design, market and launch the book. How hard could that be?

"Yep, we can do that. It'll take about 12 weeks," she told me.

"Oh great! I've booked a yacht club and our launch party is in five weeks' time. A hundred people are coming, including the Press."

tumbleweed

I thought writing the book was the hard part. Oh no, no, no! It turns out that's only half the battle.

So, what have I done differently this time? First of all, I started with a plan. I laid out some of my ideas in chapter form, so I knew what the flow of the book was going to be first, and where different stories and case studies would belong. I wouldn't have to fiddle around with the timelines on this one.

You can put the blackboard away, thank you Doc.

Next, I blocked out an entire week to write. No distractions whatsoever. I cleared the decks of all potential pitfalls, enabling me to focus every ounce of my energy on writing.

In that week, I got tens of thousands of words out of my head and onto paper. A large amount of those words never got to see the light of day, but it made the process of writing so much easier. By the end of that week, I was in flow. I had momentum on my side. I could have carried on.

But, alas, life and all its commitments were starting up again the following week and I'd be back to *squeezing in* some writing here and there.

So I got out my calendar and I put some rocks into it.

I blocked out a consecutive three-day block once a month for the following six months to focus entirely on writing this book.

A new routine. Three days per month. Every month. Without fail. Without interruption.

Six months later and you're holding this shiny new book in your hands. Something that didn't exist seven months ago – an idea born out of a simple routine.

I enjoyed the writing process a lot more this time around. I didn't feel the time pressure as I had with my last book, because I'd scheduled those rocks into the calendar well in advance.

Oh, and I didn't give my publisher a nervous breakdown this time either.

I'm still never writing another book again, though.

Then again...

Life is a rollercoaster

Over the years, I have had the following conversation with quite a few small business owners:

Business owner: "I need more work!"

Me: "Cool, here are some marketing ideas."

A month later, we'd meet up again.

Me: "How's the marketing going?"

Business owner: "Oh, I stopped doing that. I'm too busy."

Another month goes by...

Business Owner: "I need more work!"

And so the cycle continues. He needs work, so he does marketing. Marketing gets him work, so he stops marketing. Work then dries up. He goes back to marketing. Gets busy. Stops marketing. Work dries up.

My good friend and marketing consultant, Nick Jervis – NickJervis.com – has the same experience working with law firms. He calls it the Marketing Rollercoaster. In his book *'The Law Firm Growth Formula'*, Nick accurately describes the process that I've seen play out:

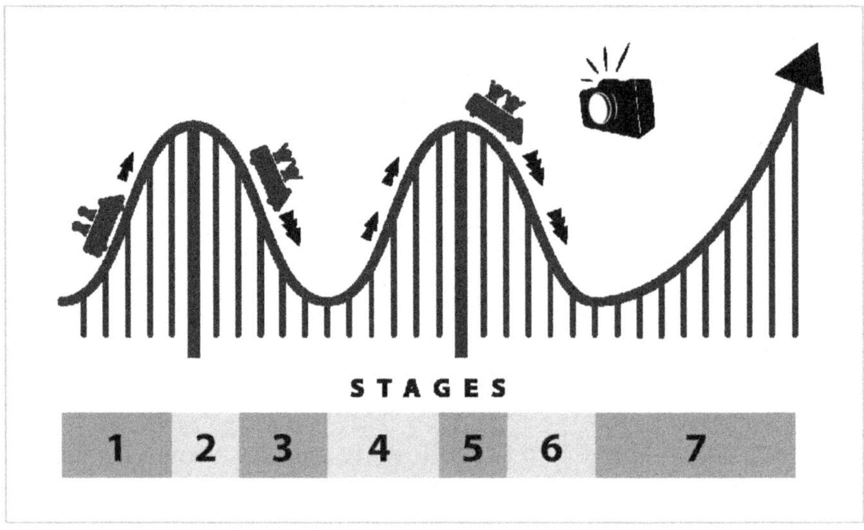

Stage 1: You have no customers. You frantically start looking for business. You contact old clients, referrers and start advertising anywhere you can think of to make your phone ring.

Stage 2: Eventually, your hard work pays off (though you are not sure what worked exactly). You have more work than you can handle, for now at least. You ease back on the marketing so that you can concentrate on the work.

Stage 3: Work starts to dwindle. You are coming down the big drop on the other side of the marketing rollercoaster and it doesn't feel good. You are sure it will pick up soon though – "word of mouth" will look after you, won't it?

Stage 4: You're back where you started, so you do what you did before and start frantically marketing.

Stages 5/6: Exactly the same thing happens again and again over the next few months. You become too busy again because of your frantic marketing activity, so you stop marketing and start heading downwards on the rollercoaster. When you reach the bottom, you start marketing again and then stop again when you reach the top. Time to put your hands in the air, scream at the top of your lungs, and smile for the camera – the big drop's coming yet again! You end up tired, bored and frustrated at your lack of progress. You decide that there has to be a better way.

Stage 7: With a strong commitment to breaking your current cycle of feast and famine, you implement a proper marketing strategy, one step at a time, until you start to see a consistent rise to success. Work keeps increasing but at a steady, predictable and manageable pace. You are not coming down the other side of the marketing rollercoaster anymore, because you are now following a proven formula.

Let's look at one such formula, shall we?

Write a swimming pool every week

It's 1964 and John Lennon and Paul McCartney are locked in a room trying to write some new songs. Their first three Beatles albums have already gone platinum, they've got six number one singles in the bag, they play to sell-out crowds every night and they have more money than they know what to do with.

So what's their motivation to keep on writing?

According to an interview with Sir Paul for Rolling Stone magazine, it was the chance to turn that writing into a swimming pool. He said: "John would be getting an extension on his house or something and the joke used to be, 'Okay! Today let's write a swimming pool'. It was great motivation.

"Then in the next three hours, 'Help!' appears from nowhere. You'd suddenly get the idea, 'This'll be a hit; this is a good one'. You become aware what you were doing was making money. Making good money."

Lennon and McCartney didn't just get lucky. They didn't write one hit song and live off the royalties for the rest of their days. They were consistent.

The Beatles were Routine Machines.

They didn't write hit songs. They wrote songs. Plenty of them. Day after day, week after week. For years. Many of them became hits, but the majority did not.

Collectively, John and Paul wrote more than 180 songs together. Some barely saw the light of day. Seventeen of them went to number one and countless more remain some of the most listened-to songs in the world, five decades after they were written.

That's more than a few swimming pools.

You may not be in a position to write yourself a new swimming pool or an extension every time you sit down with a keyboard and a blinking cursor in front of you. But there's no reason why you can't write yourself a season ticket for your favourite football team, those new shoes you've been looking at or a weekend city break.

One of the most effective marketing systems I've seen working for just about any business in recent years has been something that's so simple and yet so often overlooked.

Sending a weekly email.

One email every week to your customers, former customers and potential new customers. An email that doesn't even sell anything.

Now, you're probably wondering what the point is of sending out an email every single week that doesn't sell anything. Well, I believe marketing is simple. In my mind, it's as easy as:

1. Build a list.
2. Make friends with the list.
3. Ask for the sale.

Sending a weekly email assumes that you've done #1 and you've built a list of prospects – people who are interested in what you do. Emailing that list every week focuses on item #2 – making friends with them.

All of your effort, every single week, should be on making friends with that list – building a meaningful relationship with people who *could* do business with you to ensure that you're front of mind when they're ready to act, and priming them to be much more receptive to a sales message (#3) when you do send one.

Legendary copywriter Gary Halbert asks the following question of his students:

> *"If you and I both owned a hamburger stand and we were in a contest to see who could sell the most hamburgers, what advantages would you most like to have on your side to help you win?"*

Some students say they would like to have the advantage of the tastiest meat from which to make their burgers. Others want high-end sourdough buns. Many want to cherry-pick the best location. Someone usually wants to be able to offer the lowest prices.

After the students are finished telling him what advantages they would most like to have, Gary allows them every single one they've requested. In return, he too will have one single advantage, yet promises to outsell every last one of them.

> *"The only advantage I want," Gary says, "is a starving crowd!*
>
> *"Think about it. When it comes to direct marketing, the most profitable habit you can cultivate is the habit of constantly being on the lookout for groups of people (markets) who have demonstrated that they are starving (or at least hungry) for some particular product or service."*

Weekly emails *create* a starving crowd.

By sending one solitary email every single week for a prolonged period of time, and by not even attempting to sell anything in it, you'll start getting emails like this:

"I want in!!!"

"When do the doors open?"

"Fully aware next intake isn't until March... Sob!"

Those are actual replies that I've just copied and pasted from my inbox. People who want to join the One Percent Club outside of our twice-yearly intakes.

As I write this, we're six weeks away from the doors being open, and I'm not even thinking about writing any sales messages yet. I've just been sending weekly "make friends" emails consistently, demonstrating that I know my stuff, giving a little bit of value, educating a tiny bit, showing a minute piece of the full service that you'd get as a One Percenter.

And look at the effect it has. It creates a starving crowd of people who want to buy even though I'm not selling anything yet!

We usually open the doors to the One Percent Club in March and September, so anyone interested in joining has either 30 or 31 days to make the decision and commit.

Every time, roughly a third of new One Percenters join in the last 48 hours of the month. Deadlines get people to take action. Another third will sign up between days four and 28. They respond well to the sales messages that I send out during the sales window.

The final third join almost immediately I open the doors and certainly within the first 48 hours. The minute I open the doors, I get a flood of applications from small business owners wanting to grow their business.

That sounds like a starving crowd to me!

Looking back over the last few years of data for the One Percent Club, the "starving crowd" members tend to be some of our best members too – they interact more, they're more likely to actually implement what we teach and they tend to stick around for years. They're great for the One Percent Club and the One Percent Club is great for them.

Taking a few months to "make friends" with them via a weekly email pays huge dividends later down the line when we eventually do ask for the sale.

This works brilliantly for us. It works brilliantly for some of our One Percenters. And it will work brilliantly for you.

Puttin' on the Ritz

Carolyne Wahlen from Gap HR started emailing a cold list of potential clients in the hospitality sector around a year ago. Here's what she said about it:

> *"Ninety-nine per cent of the people on the list didn't know me until I started talking to them. I've been emailing them once a week for a year now. I only sell twice a year, in January and June. I've just done our January sales campaign and achieved a 50 per cent conversion rate with 14 warm leads.*
>
> *Because I've not been selling to them, I've just been entertaining them for months and months, when I do finally have something to sell them our conversion rate is 50 per cent.*
>
> *One lady responded to the sales campaign and I asked if she could do a call at 2pm on Monday, and she replied: "What time zone?" This made me check what company she worked for. It was The Leading Hotels of the World. They have The Ritz! She was in New York and wanted me to evaluate their UK documents. Wow! And all because, as she said, she loves my emails and I have built up trust.*
>
> *I get lots of leads outside of the sales window too, just from doing the weekly emails, despite the fact they're not selling in any way. HR is very reactive, so clients don't tend to contact me until they're in pain. But I'm the one who's in their email inbox every single week, whose emails they actually read every week, and so when they do have a HR issue, I'm the person who gets the call.*

I treat my weekly emails as a therapy session. I rant about everything and then ask a copywriter to turn it into an entertaining rant. I usually write about something HR-related, but put a personal spin or story attached to it."

Carolyne has earned the right to sell because she's attracted the eyeballs and the attention to her weekly emails by sending valuable content each and every week. She's created the starving crowd and then offered to feed them twice a year.

There's another Routine Machine lesson here. Carolyne created the original sales campaign in 2016 and because it works so well, she's simply rinsed and repeated it twice a year ever since.

Carolyne is a Routine Machine.

HR can be quite a dry, boring subject (apologies to Carolyne and an army of other HR people who I've just offended), but Carolyne's emails are anything but boring. You don't have to write amazing, Pulitzer-prize-winning content. You just have to be "not boring" and a little bit entertaining.

The £350,000 phone call

Paul Bleck, from Bartech Marine Engineering, started sending weekly emails almost three years ago. He said:

"The email list we started off with was just people who had submitted an enquiry at some point in the past – probably a couple of thousand people. We've built that list up primarily through LinkedIn, which is very useful for finding the right people in the right sectors, and we've now got almost 10,000 people getting our weekly emails.

Our weekly emails are usually about something that's come up that week.

Because we're targeting engineers, we talk about something that our engineers have found out on-site or a job that's come into the workshop. Because we work on this kind of stuff every day, we see lots of different situations and can talk about what the root causes are, what the tell-tale signs could be and what the person reading the email could do to protect themselves.

An engineer on a ship wouldn't necessarily see these problems regularly, so they find our content quite interesting and, for us, we're seen as the experts – it enables us to demonstrate the breadth of experience that we have.

We don't do any selling in the weekly emails whatsoever, but we still pick up clients as a result. We had one such client receive our emails every week for almost two years before hitting reply and saying, "'We've got an upcoming overhaul. Could you quote for it please?' We won the contract and that single client alone has been worth more than £350,000 so far.

That's £350k purely by connecting with them, building up the confidence week-by-week, demonstrating how we do things through the content of our emails, and nurturing that relationship. They've turned out to be an ideal client of ours.

We get a lot of positive feedback from the emails; people always comment on the latest email or tell me that they've been reading them for the last six months. It's also been a fantastic tool for recruiting really good members of staff, as the weekly emails give an insight into what it's like to work at Bartech.

We also repurpose the content, so as well as sending it out via email, we'll post it on LinkedIn, Facebook and Twitter. It's the same content, but just going out to different audiences. The content I pasted onto LinkedIn yesterday has already been viewed more than 4,000 times!"

Like Carolyne, Paul works in a responsive industry. His phone only tends to ring when things break!

By being in the inboxes (or LinkedIn, Facebook or Twitter feeds) of the right people every single week, he's front of mind when things *do* break so it's his phone that rings, not that of his competitors. And when contracts are worth up to £350,000, that's a phone call you want to take!

Tender is the touch...

Ben Wheeler, from Copper Bay Creative, had to have his arm twisted to start sending weekly emails. He told me:

"I resisted sending weekly emails for a long, long time until I was held accountable to do it. I always seemed to have 'more important' things to be doing than to send an email out that didn't even sell anything.

I've been sending them out for around six months now and it's now one of the best pieces of marketing we do.

Over Christmas, there was a tender from a county council. It was released on a Friday with the deadline being the following Monday. I presumed it was a done deal, merely 'ticking the box' and that it had already been decided who was going to win the tender.

For some reason, though, I decided to go ahead anyway and submitted my bid, which took me around 20 minutes. I was notified on the Monday that I had been shortlisted and invited in for a meeting.

I duly went to the meeting, where I was introduced to the panel as: 'This is Ben. He's going to be doing our website.'

I'd won the tender before I'd even opened my mouth. I couldn't figure out how it had been so easy.

And then I popped the decision maker's email address into my CRM only to find it was already there. She'd been getting, opening and reading every single one of my weekly emails for the last four months.

They've already spent £6,000 with me, but have committed to a three-year deal which will be worth in the region of £30,000 to £40,000.

Three or four times per month now, I'm getting replies to my emails (which I don't sell through), asking me to quote for work. It's definitely worth doing."

By the time Ben physically appeared in front of her (and her team), this person felt that she already knew him. Her decision was made. She was starving and "burger boy" turned up with the smell of sizzling onions filling the meeting room.

It was easy to sell Ben to her team and to her superiors – "This is the guy I was telling you about. I know everything about him, what he can do, and how he works." It's so much easier for her to trust that Ben will be consistent with her experience of him over the last four months than it is to take a punt on someone unknown who may have written a better pitch.

By sending weekly emails, you're front of mind when people are ready to buy. You're never more than six days away from making contact with them again. You build trust. You demonstrate expertise. You craft a relationship. You create a starving crowd. And that could be all the advantage you need.

Staring at a blinking cursor?

One of the biggest objections I hear from people when I advise them to start sending weekly emails is that they don't know what to write about.

I get it. I write for a living – I write books, I write copy, I write emails, I write social media posts and I write sales letters. I probably spend 80 per cent of my working life arse in chair, hands on keyboard.

I know that there are few things more demoralising to the aspiring writer than to stare at a blank document with a blinking cursor taunting you. So what do you write about?

Well, Carolyne starts by thinking about things that have annoyed her recently. Writing it out is cheap therapy that her copywriter then polishes up into a nice weekly email.

Paul spots opportunities to share unusual stories and case studies from his everyday work.

Ben likes to write about mistakes he sees businesses making with their websites.

These are all good places to start because they show that you're able to spot bad practice in your sector (which automatically elevates you to "good" status). Talking about your own industry to an audience that also has an interest in your sector is a no-brainer. But you shouldn't just talk shop.

There's nothing more boring than an accountant trying to do weekly emails and sending out a weekly diatribe of the latest updates to the tax code, the importance of double-entry bookkeeping or how to file your receipts and invoices in a more efficient manner.

When the news is full of Starbucks and Amazon paying hardly any tax, MP expenses scandals, the Sunday Times Rich List, and so on, this is what the general public are interested in and it is very easy for the accountant to talk about a hot news item, but simply put a spin on the story that relates to their firm or their customers.

Remember, the aim of the weekly emails is *not* to sell. It's to build rapport, to grow your reputation as an expert and to nurture a relationship with your customers and prospects. And the best way to do that is to get a bit personal.

Share some of *you* with your readers.

Regular readers of my weekly emails know a hell of a lot about me. They know I've got two young boys. They know I'm a Plymouth Argyle fan. They know I've recently had a puppy join our household. They know where I went on holiday last year and where I'm going next year.

They know that I'm learning to play golf, that I go to the gym and that I'm very particular about my coffee. They know my wife's a teacher and that I love eating cake.

They know all this, yet they didn't sign up for my weekly emails because they wanted to stalk me and find out what I had for tea last night (slow-cooked Moroccan lamb, since you asked). No, they want to get my weekly emails for the business lessons and marketing ideas that are contained within them.

And there are a shed-load of "knowledge-bombs" and educational value in my weekly emails. But in order to educate, I first have to overcome a pretty major hurdle. I have to get my emails opened and read. So they need to be entertaining, as well as containing useful information.

Infotaining, you could say.

So I tell a lot of stories. I share good things (and bad things) that I see from the world of marketing and small business. I'll talk about how making one tiny change to my golf swing made *all* the difference and how that principle applies to business too.

There's a magic phrase that will help you to write infotaining copy: "And [YOUR SECTOR] is a bit like that too."

Start with an interesting story and then relate that story to your sector, your business or your customers. For example:

> *"I was running late today and forgot to de-ice my car. I couldn't find the ice-scraper that Aunt Lillian bought me for Christmas last year, so I grabbed the first thing that came to hand – an old Coldplay CD. It did the job but it took me three times as long as Aunt Lillian's device would have done and Chris Martin doesn't quite sound the same anymore.*
>
> *And [YOUR SECTOR] is a bit like that too.*
>
> *You might be using something that's not fit for purpose. Sure, it does the job, but only just. I see people all the time, using X to do Y. It takes them so much longer and costs them so much more money in the long run."*

Keep one eye on the trending stories on your favourite news website and see how you can leverage those stories in your next weekly email. Don't just focus on your sector. Look for interesting stories. I like the "most watched" section of the BBC News website. This shows me what people are *actually* interested in. As I write this, some of the most popular stories on there include:

- Women caught putting hair on pub pizza.
- What this Michelin-starred chef wants to change.
- Has Trump kept his promises?
- Do children in two-parent families do better?
- How tuition fees change real-life decisions.

No matter what the sector, I would be confident in turning any of these stories into an infotaining email that somehow relates to my business. Ignore the specifics about each story and look at the general topics:

- People trying to cheat the system. Customers lying to you.
- Thinking outside the box. Embracing change.
- Keeping promises. Being divisive.
- What does it take to succeed? Parenting.
- What drives behaviour? Pricing.

If you're struggling to find industry-specific topics, start with a human story first. Something everyone can relate to such as the unbridled joy of landing a scrunched-up bit of paper in the bin from the other side of the room, the pain of bare feet meeting LEGO, asking why cabbage doesn't taste as good as cake or how kids seem to have selective hearing.

I send out a new email to the people on my list every Wednesday lunchtime, as regular as clockwork (like a Routine Machine). It's a bit like getting a bonus book chapter from me each week.

And I guarantee readers learn something – even if it's just how Plymouth Argyle are faring or whether carrot cake or salad is my food of choice at that moment in time.

Homework

Question: What's your equivalent "swimming pool" that you'd like to write?

Task: Start sending weekly emails. If you want to see an example or two, you can view mine (including old ones) at:

- www.bigidea.co.uk

9. IF THIS, THEN THAT

We all want to be more productive, healthier, build better relationships with loved ones, earn more money, and look and feel like a million dollars.

Becoming a Routine Machine can get you there.

We've got the best of intentions, but we need a little help creating those routines. Good news – there's an app for that.

Want to walk 10,000 steps a day? Strap on a Fitbit and track those strides. Need to remember to call your parents every other day? Set a recurring reminder on your phone.

Keen to give up smoking? Download an app that'll tell you how many cancer sticks you haven't smoked, how much money you've saved and how much longer you're going to live.

Want to replace drive-time DJs with inspiring people and creative ideas on your daily commute? Hook your car up to Bluetooth and stream audiobooks and podcasts instead.

Looking to improve your memory? Download some games that are proven to improve cognitive skills.

Always wanted to be able to do 100 push-ups? There's an app that will coach you from doing one to 100, all via a daily routine.

When you start a new routine, the process isn't going to be automatic. The Human has to override the Computer each time, as you've learned. But there's no reason why the Human can't get some help from another computer.

The key to turning any new routine into an established habit lies in the automation. Manually repeat the same action enough times and the Computer writes a script to handle it on autopilot in the future. So why not use the technology available to you in your laptop or smartphone to set up some computer-led automation from day one?

Technology is your friend.

Here are three of my current "couldn't live without" pieces of tech that help my daily routines work on autopilot:

- **Braintoss**
  I have most of my creative ideas when I'm either sat in the sauna or out walking with the dogs rather than when I'm sat at my desk in front of my laptop or with my trusty notebook to hand.

  Luckily, I have Braintoss, which is a simple app that records a 30-second piece of dictation, a typed note or an image, photo or screenshot and emails it to me.

  That's it! It enables me to stop, quickly capture the amazing idea before it vanishes forever, and send it to my inbox for me to look at when I *am* sat in front of my laptop.

- **Audible/podcasts**
  I used to listen to music every time I got in the car. What a waste of a drive. Then, a few years ago, I discovered the joy of audiobooks and podcasts. Now I look at a three-hour drive from Plymouth to Birmingham as an opportunity to devour an entire book in one sitting.

  My car has become a mobile library. Three hours each way is six hours sat in "the library" devouring inspirational content, brilliant new ideas and strategies, and studying the blueprints of those who have walked before me.

  Listening on 1.3-times speed also means that I can digest almost eight hours of content in a single Plymouth-Birmingham round trip. That's like an entire day-long seminar happening in my car with the world's greatest speakers lined up, spilling their secrets, and all in that "dead-time" that I'd have otherwise wasted just plodding up and down the M5.

I prefer podcasts when driving and audiobooks when walking the dogs. You see, I don't walk the dogs on my own. I take Tony Robbins with me. Or Ray Dalio. Or Jordan Belfort. Sir Richard Branson, Arnold Schwarzenegger and Sir Alex Ferguson have also been known to accompany me on my daily dog walks, too.

- **Calendar**

  If it's not in my calendar, it doesn't exist. My online calendar runs my life. I've got automated alerts and alarms set up so I get a text message (and an email and usually an Alexa audio reminder too) ten minutes before Harry needs picking up from gym club on a Wednesday or that Jack's 11+ tutor arrives on a Tuesday.

  I've got recurring alerts to remind me each week to post on social media and to send "monthly update" marketing emails each month. Every recurring task that needs to happen in each of my businesses has a corresponding, recurring alert set up to nudge and notify the team member responsible.

  Jason and I have a shared calendar, where all our One Percent Club coaching calls, masterclasses and Ambitious. Lifestyle. Business. Podcast recordings are batched and planned out two or three months in advance.

  Every Plymouth Argyle home game for the season is pre-loaded in there, as well as every holiday, appointment and meeting that is already planned for the foreseeable future.

But – and here's the important bit – what goes into my calendar first?

You should remember from earlier in the book that the correct answer is the immovable objects – my rocks.

Well, guess what? Because I've automated the recurring alerts for the really important stuff, those immovable objects automatically go into my calendar first.

He's not the Messiah. He's a very naughty boy

In February 2006, my beloved Plymouth Argyle signed Cameroonian striker Vincent Péricard on loan from rivals Portsmouth. In his first match, Péricard scored a hat-trick against Coventry City in a 3-1 win for the Pilgrims.

I thought we'd uncovered a real gem – that much-sought-after 20 goals a season striker, who would surely propel us up the table towards the promised land of the Premier League. A hat-trick in your first game? The boy's clearly got class and will be banging them in left, right and centre for the rest of the season. He'll pick up the Player of the Year award and go on to have legendary status at the club alongside Tommy Tynan, Paul Mariner and Mickey Evans.

Or not.

Péricard actually spent the following 14 games falling over a lot, sitting on his arse, complaining to the referee and gesticulating to his teammates that his failure to score was somehow their fault. He scored one more goal in those 14 matches.

Three goals in one match and then one goal in 14.

Vincent Péricard was not a Routine Machine. He was not the Messiah. He was a very naughty boy (Péricard was caught doing 103mph on the A38 near Plymouth, then lied to police by claiming his stepfather was at the wheel, and was sentenced to four months in prison for perverting the course of justice).

What's tougher, hitting a home run or hitting a .342 batting average over your entire career as Babe Ruth did? Is it harder to hole a single 50-yard putt or sink 99.81 per cent of all three-yard putts, as Tiger Woods has to date? Scoring a hat-trick for Plymouth Argyle in one game or scoring 238 goals in 460 games like Gary Lineker did during his playing days?

Almost anyone can be a world-beater on any given day. You already have "world-beater" days where you smash out a fantastic gym session, eat really well or complete some amazing work. Three goals in one game standard.

But do you then revert to form? Back to your one goal in 14 level?

If so, then you need to summon your inner Babe Ruth. Shift the focus from this next shot, the next day, the next piece of work or the next goal in front of you and instead focus on maintaining and improving your average.

There are not many personal development books that will advise you to focus on being average, but that's exactly what I'm going to prescribe now. It's how you're going to become a Routine Machine.

Here's how.

Create a spreadsheet. Along the top row, list everything you want to track (such as your health, family, stress levels, work, personal development, etc.).

Next, add fields in the first column for each individual day. Then score yourself from one to ten for each area, every single day. A PB at the gym scores you a ten for fitness, but a KFC for lunch might see your nutrition drop to five and a half. Did you forget to meditate today? Oops, that's a zero for mindfulness.

Now, here's the crucial part. Create a formula within the spreadsheet that adds up all your scores and tells you your 30-day average, your 60-day average and your 90-day average.

Don't worry if you don't know how to do this, you'll find a spreadsheet with the formulas already in place in the resources section at the end of the book.

Your spreadsheet should look something like this:

	Health	Family	Stress	Sleep	Work	Mindfulness	Personal Dev
30 day average	7.58	7.24	8.55	9.11	5.67	8.57	8.77
60 day average	7.94	7.77	8.95	9.01	7.66	8.99	8.12
90 day average	7.88	7.56	8.91	9.01	7.94	8.67	8.09
Day 1	4.6	8	6	8	7	8	5
Day 2	3.5	5.5	7	7.5	1.5	5	8
Day 3	6.5	6	8	7	7	7	4
Day 4	9.5	10	8	9	10	8	7.5
Day 5	8	8.5	8	8	8	7.5	10

And now you can focus on just one thing – increasing your average. You no longer try to score hat-tricks, sink 50-yard putts or hit home runs. You just need to maintain and improve your running averages in the areas that matter to you.

What's going to get you fitter, running a marathon once or maintaining a 90-day average of 9.24 for health?

How can you be a better parent? Buy your kids an iPad for Christmas or keep your 60-day average above 8.5 by coming home from work on time, eating meals together and talking to them regularly?

What you do today doesn't matter. What you did yesterday didn't matter. What you do tomorrow won't matter. But what you do every day, consistently for 30, 60 or 90 days matters a lot.

You now have my permission to be average.

I wish it could be Christmas every day... but my belly doesn't

I've had some health goals on my vision board for the last couple of years. Now, I'm not looking to drop a massive amount of weight or take up bodybuilding, but I do want to lose a few more pounds and a few more inches (don't we all).

So every year I set myself the goal of getting to a certain waist measurement and a certain body fat percentage.

And every year I achieve that goal.

For about a week.

It's usually just before the summer holidays (yes, the pressure of being "beach body ready" works on me) when I'll then proceed to spend the following six weeks eating my body weight in ice cream and end up gaining another stone, which I'll then slowly lose over the next three months, getting back to my goal once again just in time for...

Christmas.

Mince pies. Christmas cake. Clotted cream. A tub of chocolates for breakfast. Eating plates full of cold meat and cheese for days on end even though you're not hungry. Good times.

By the time January rolls around, my waist measurements would rival Father Christmas himself and I'm ready to get back on the green juices. I'm literally craving salads and vegetables and, sure enough, I don't find it too hard to lose the festive excess by just getting back into my usual routine.

You see, what I eat between Christmas and New Year doesn't have anywhere near as much impact as what I eat between New Year and Christmas.

For the last few years, I've used an app called My Fitness Pal to log my weight, waist measurements and body fat percentage.

Take a look at the following chart and see if you can spot where Christmas might have happened:

Oops.

So, I want to change the habit of a lifetime and not gain a shedload of weight over Christmas. How am I going to do that?

If I want a different result, I'm going to need a different routine.

As well as logging my measurements, I can also use the app to log what food I eat and break that down into macronutrients and micronutrients. Macronutrients (or macros) are the main food groups – proteins, fats and carbohydrates.

Micronutrients (or micros) are the more specific vitamins and minerals contained within the food, such as vitamin A, calcium, fibre, sodium, potassium, iron and so on.

I discovered recently that the simple act of telling this app what food I put in my mouth actually controls what I choose to put in my mouth. Now, no one is looking at this data other than me and the only person I'm accountable to is myself. But the sheer fact that I know eating that Mars bar means I have to tell the app that I just ate 40 per cent of my daily allowance of carbs in one sitting, along with 35 grams of sugar.

The routine of logging what food I eat makes it easier to say no to Mars bars. It's no longer an emotional decision (I really, really want a Mars bar). It's been turned into a logical decision ("You *can* have a Mars bar. Here's what it's going to cost you. Would you like to proceed?").

This Christmas, I will log every single item that I put into my mouth. Every slice of turkey. Every pig in blanket. Every Brussels sprout.

Shall I have a couple of chocolates? Let me see. Three Quality Street chocolates (which may be the contents of an entire tub in a few Christmases time) will cost me 132 calories and 19 grams of carbs. And I'm not even hungry! Pass me a nectarine or some of those walnuts.

Playing with my food

When you make a change to any routine, you never get instant feedback. It's always weeks, months or sometimes years down the line before you see the results. You can't give up smoking today and start your Olympic sprinting career tomorrow.

Using an app like My Fitness Pal enables me to see what happens when I play with my food. I can try out a really high-fat diet where I'm blending butter into my coffee for a month and then track the results. I can see what happens to my body fat percentage when I massively dial up my protein intake.

If you look back at my Christmas graph above, you'll see what happens when I have a big spike in carbs for two weeks. I wouldn't advise that as a long-term diet plan!

I can play with the macros. I can set myself targets of how much of each macronutrient to consume each day and adjust the food I eat to deliver that.

If I want to, I can get really specific and also play with the micronutrients. If I've got an iron deficiency, I can target iron-rich foods. If I find I'm not getting enough sodium or vitamin C, then I can set those as targets too.

I can see what happens four weeks after I treble my intake of fibre or halve my daily sugar levels. It's almost like a game. Everything you put in your mouth affects almost all of the macros and all of the micros.

Butter will deliver you a big hit of fat with zero carbs. But it's calorific. A protein shake will help you hit your protein goals, but contains next to no fibre. A Mars bar is full of carbs, but will give you 10g of fat and 3g of protein too. Sprouts and cabbage are great sources of micronutrients, but I still can't stand them.

You don't have to just play with your food either, you can apply macros and micros to just about any routine that you want to change.

Want to improve your work/life balance? Dial up your "spending time with the family" macro and turn down "staying late at the office".

Need to make more money? Increase your marketing macros and cut back on the "unnecessary spending" macronutrient.

Getting stressed all the time? Eat foods rich in mindfulness and avoid drinking pints of "hanging around with idiots".

Whatever you want to achieve, there are macros that you can dial up and dial down. This might sound overly simplistic, but it really isn't much more difficult than doing more of what helps and less of what hinders.

Fewer Mars bars and more broccoli.

Adjust your macros and monitor the results in the long term. The more you change your macros, the more change you'll see.

What if your macros are already spot on? If you've already optimised your macros, then it's time to get micro. It's time to get really specific and start sweating the small stuff.

So you want to make more money in your business and you've optimised all your macros in terms of "working on the business versus in the business"?

Great, time to get micro. Time to dial up/down on some of the following:

- Pricing.
- Social media.
- Customer service.
- Conversion rates.
- Customer retention.
- Search engine optimisation.
- Staff training.
- PR.
- Upsells.
- Referrals.
- Buying competitors.
- Your learning.
- Hiring a coach or mentor.
- Mindfulness.
- Personal development.
- Systems and processes.
- HR.
- Accounting.
- Admin.
- Copywriting.

- Lead generation.
- Web design.
- Print design.
- Networking.
- And about three million other things.

Try to get a feel for how much of each of these micronutrients you're currently getting in your business and where you feel you're lacking.

So many people tell me that they've overdosing on admin and obsessing over accounts, when the real problem is that they're deficient in lead generation, not getting anywhere near enough systems and processes, and have a chronic lack of personal development.

Give yourself a score out of 20 for each of the items in that list and you'll start to see where you might want to direct your attention and create a new routine. That's not to say you have to take every item to a 20. Just as you may not care how much potassium you eat every day, this is just a marker to show you where you actually are right now.

And you can use that marker to decide what to target next. If you want different numbers, you need different routines.

If you spot that one area is particularly low, you can divert your attention there, dial up (or down) the micros in that area and track the results further down the line.

Make sure you're looking at the measurements that actually matter though. When it comes to my fitness, it's the tape measure result that ultimately matters for me. Not weight, BMI, body fat percentage, etc.

I want to know when my belly's getting a bit too wobbly and would ideally like to see a hint of abs underneath the blubber when I take my shirt off. The tape measure monitors that nicely for me.

I recently lost five per cent of my body fat overnight. How did I achieve this amazing feat? Was it a crash diet? A gastric band? Liposuction? A particularly bad stomach bug?

Nope. I simply bought a different set of scales. The tape measure didn't move, as I hadn't really lost this fat at all, and it helped me realise the measurements that really matter.

It's the same with our businesses. Return on investment (ROI) is pretty much the only measurement that matters. We put together a 23-page KPI (key performance indicator) report each and every month. But the clickthrough rates, email open rates, Twitter engagement numbers and bounce rates ultimately don't matter. What matters is the ROI.

Of course, all of those other factors contribute to the ROI, but they're micro and I want to really focus on moving the macro number. That should be where all my strategic efforts go.

And while technology can help build your Routine Machine and is fantastic for monitoring, measuring, and reminding, it's also worth remembering that it's not without its pitfalls.

Take the red pill

"Please remain seated with your seatbelt fastened until the plane has come to a complete stop and the captain has turned off the overhead seatbelt signs."

Our plane touched down at Corfu International Airport after an uneventful three and a half hour flight from Bristol. The local time was 8.15am and 6.15am back in the UK.

The silence in the cabin was immediately replaced by a cacophony of rebellious passengers ignoring the cabin crew's request to leave their seatbelts alone for a further 37 seconds, and instead unbuckling themselves in a bid to hit the beaches and bars of Corfu town those precious few seconds sooner.

Freed of their lap constraints, all eyes were on the seatbelt signs.

Wait for it.

Wait for it.

ding

Two hundred and fifty people stand in unison, grab their hand luggage, face their nearest exit (which may be behind you) and wait.

And wait.

Five minutes pass and we were all standing there in the aisle, trying to avoid making eye contact with anyone (Tube rules apply here).

How on earth are we supposed to fill those five minutes? Ah, I know. Let's power up the mobile and get on the local 3G network.

"Welcome to Greece. Call & text UK, EU and other EEA numbers, and get online using your allowance at no extra cost here."

Safely connected to the net once again, I load up Facebook and check my notifications. There aren't any.

"That's weird," I think. And then I remember two things.

1. It's 6.15am on a Saturday morning back in the UK. I last checked Facebook before take-off around 3am. Not much happens in the UK in the middle of the night and what does happen probably shouldn't be posted on Facebook.

2. I'm supposed to be on holiday. I'm here with the family to enjoy a break from work. Facebook is work. The internet is work.

I haven't flown 1,400 miles to sit on Facebook and check emails. I'm here to have fun, to swim, to explore, to laugh, to eat, to jet-ski and to relax.

So I turn my mobile data off. I unplug myself from the IV drip of access to the internet. For someone who works on the net and has built a life around online marketing for the best part of 20 years, this is tough to do.

But the minute I make that decision, I know I've done the right thing. I can actually be present with the people I love for the entire duration of the next two weeks, actually having conversations with each other, talking about our hopes and dreams, laughing together, playing games, and splashing around in the pool.

When you go on holiday (or go to a gig or a wedding or a party), are you actually present? Are you really there or are you just watching your life through the screen of your phone? Do you have actual memories of these events or just the photos and videos that your phone captured?

Next time you go to a gig, pay attention to how many people spend the entire show "watching" the band through their phone. These people have paid a decent chunk of change to see their favourite band play up close and personal, but then watch their heroes perform through a five-inch screen.

After a few days of my self-imposed digital detox, I had recovered from the withdrawal symptoms. I'd got over the shakes and no longer woke in the middle of the night imagining that I'd heard an important notification come in.

I could actually feel my stress levels dropping by order of magnitude. I was like Neo in the Matrix films, suddenly aware of "the system" and the automatons that it creates. Every time I skipped merrily through the hotel reception en route to creating more amazing memories with those I love, I saw miserable faces everywhere – all staring into their phones.

There were entire families not saying a word to each other, avoiding eye contact and with faces like a bulldog sucking on a lemon-flavoured wasp, but still "liking" each other's highly filtered and staged photos on Instagram.

They were plugged into the Matrix, but I'd taken the red pill.

Sure, I did have to "plug in" a few times while I was away. I have designed my businesses to run without me, but they don't thrive without me (yet!). So I blocked out a two-hour window each week, connected to the hotel wifi, grabbed a cappuccino and did two hours of focused work.

Then I unplugged again and headed to the spa. Or hired a pedalo. Or went for a swim in the sea. None of which I needed my phone for. My mobile spent a fortnight locked in a safe.

I'd release it at night to use a white noise app, which helps me to sleep better, to sync my daily steps from my Fitbit, and to set an alarm for the following day. At 10pm, I'd still have 95 per cent battery remaining.

We always debrief our holidays as a family once we get back to Blighty. While sat in Gourmet Burger Kitchen slurping on a salted caramel milkshake (the healthy eating routine started the next day), we all agreed that our fortnight in Corfu had been the best holiday we'd ever had.

Let me repeat that. We all agreed.

We never agree. I like to sit by the pool and do nothing but read my Kindle for two weeks. Sarah likes to hire a car and go exploring. Jack wants to stay indoors doing arts and crafts, and Harry wants to splash around on the beach.

We did all that and more, because we were actually present. We took the red pill, unplugged from the system and enjoyed two weeks of blissful, quality family time.

If you think you might like to take the red pill a little more often (not just on family holidays), here are a few things you could try:

- Turn mobile data off when on holiday.
- Turn your phone off when doing focused work.
- Don't get your phone out at gigs.
- Put your phone in aeroplane mode after 9pm every day.
- Put your phone in another room when you sleep.
- Delete any apps that are time vampires or fuel negative routines.
- Install apps that restrict the amount of time you can spend on social media.
- Have "screen-free Saturdays".
- Don't answer your phone unless you've booked in the call (or it's an emergency).
- Ban screens from the dinner table.
- When you're with somebody and your phone buzzes, don't check the notification. Use it as an anchor, to make eye contact with the other person and be truly present with them.
- Turn off most notifications on your phone. This is the first thing I do when I get a new phone. My phone notifies me

> of text messages, calendar reminders and phone calls. That's it. I want to control my phone, not the other way around.

Your mobile phone should be an amazing tool that serves you. It should help you build positive routines that help you to achieve your goals. In order to do that, though, you're going to need to limit its powers somewhat, especially if you find that you are constantly responding to its requests, rather than it to yours.

Take the red pill.

Homework

Task: Find one app that helps build positive routines and start using it. Find one app on your phone that fuels negative routines and delete it.

Task: Create a spreadsheet and track your 30, 60 and 90-day averages for the areas you want to improve. You'll find details on how to get a ready-made spreadsheet with all the formulas in place in the resources section at the end of the book.

10. HOW DO YOU FIND THE TIME?

I've been coaching small business owners for a good few years now, advising them on how to market their businesses better and how to design their businesses around the lifestyle that they'd like to lead.

A common complaint I hear from new people we start to work with is: "I don't have time for this. I'm far too busy as it is."

Now, I could understand if they were busy running local government or managing a team of 15. But most of these guys are one-man bands and are just busy doing "stuff".

If they were to go through the time audit process, I bet they'd discover that they spend 40 per cent of their time doing client work and 60 per cent just faffing around.

I recall a conversation with a One Percenter who sold her time by the hour. We started talking about how to market her business more effectively, which involved her speaking on stage and then following up with leads from the attendees. It was a model she'd accidentally stumbled upon and had already given her seven hot prospects from one 30-minute talk.

My advice was simple. Do that again. Do it every month or every quarter. Do it routinely.

"I haven't got time to do that," she said.

"Can I see your diary?" I asked.

"What do you mean? Why do you need to see my diary?"

"Well, last time we spoke you told me that you could sell 30 hours per week to clients and spend ten hours per week marketing for new clients. That was your capacity?"

"That's right."

"Well, I think it's great that you're now selling 30 hours a week and have filled your diary."

"But I haven't filled my diary."

"So how many hours have you sold to clients next week?"

"About ten."

"So you've got 30 hours free to spend on marketing then?"

"No, I told you. I'm too busy!"

"Busy doing what?"

"Erm..."

This is something that I see repeated again and again with business owners all over the country, especially with one-man bands (or one-lady bands).

Because they've fallen into the habit of doing everything themselves and becoming a jack-of-all-trades, they've become so used to just being busy day after day, week after week, without consciously thinking about *what* they're actually busy doing. It's just another day at the coal face for them.

I'm not in their business, of course, so I'm able to see the bigger picture very easily and focus on their business. I can see how all the moving parts work and get the "helicopter view" on what the current state of play is and what needs to change.

You are now Anneka Rice

Remember the TV game show Treasure Hunt? Contestants would have to solve cryptic puzzles and study maps in a race against the clock to find and solve clues, which would be in different parts of the UK countryside. Once they'd solved a particular clue, it would give them the location of the next puzzle, which could be several miles away.

At this point, a jumpsuit-clad Anneka Rice would leap into a waiting helicopter, the pilot would get permission to fly and they'd be off.

The contestants would then start to debate what the clues could mean. They could use what little knowledge they might have of the area, but they also had local history books, encyclopaedias, maps and other reference books available to them. Sadly, they didn't yet have access to Google.

Often, the key that unlocked a particular clue was Anneka shouting from her 5,000ft vantage position, "I can see a stream next to an old factory," or "I'm following the path of the railway, and there seems to be a radio tower next to the industrial estate."

Because she was 5,000ft up and able to see for miles in every direction, Anneka had an advantage over the contestants in the studio. She had a "helicopter view". She was able to spot a potential opportunity, fly a few miles towards it, descend to get a closer look and then either confirm whether it was what they were looking for or rule it out.

She could see things from her helicopter viewpoint that she would never have noticed had she been on the ground.

If you can't see the wood for the trees, then maybe you should put on a jumpsuit and embrace your inner-Anneka. Hop into your metaphorical helicopter and take it up to 5,000ft, get above those trees and buildings, look down on your business, on your health or your lifestyle – whatever you want to change – and see how different everything looks from up there.

It is just like when you take off in an aeroplane and notice how small the people, houses and cars look after a minute or two. You suddenly notice the contours of the countryside, the way the motorways snake through the hills, and how the towns and villages are packed together in pockets of green open space.

Things look very different from up here.

Getting a helicopter view of things makes it more obvious what your life *actually* looks like. You can picture what the landscape *could* look like if you moved things around and did certain things differently. You can see how all the working parts fit together. You can spot which parts need replacing, which processes aren't working optimally, which buildings need knocking down, and where the opportunities are.

You can't see any of this if you're stuck at ground level constantly. If you're stuck in the day-to-day, you're on that hamster wheel just focusing on the next thing that lands on your desk. You're in the dense woodland of your daily life, but you can't see the wood for the trees.

Zip up your jumpsuit and hop in the chopper – we've got permission to take off. It's time to get above the trees and get a good helicopter view on your life.

You can't 'find' time

If you are the sort of person who seems to achieve a lot, then you'll no doubt be asked the following question on a regular basis: "How do you find the time?"

On the surface, that would appear to be a perfectly good question. "You seem to achieve a lot more than me, so I'd like to know where you're finding the time to do that. I've filled every hour of every day and feel I physically couldn't fit any more in. Therefore, you must have discovered a 25th hour in the day. It's the only logical answer."

Well, I'm sorry to burst your bubble, but I have yet to discover that elusive 25th hour. Anneka Rice is still hovering above East Anglia somewhere hunting for it and I'll be sure to let you know the moment she finds it. But for now, we're all stuck with a measly 24 hours per day.

Sara Blakely has 24 hours in a day and she "found the time" to become the youngest self-made female billionaire in US history.

Bill Gates is stuck with just 24 hours a day, yet he "finds the time" to try to rid the world of polio, HIV and malaria.

Elon Musk is also limited to a mere 24 hours per day and he "finds the time" to make self-driving cars and build rockets that will enable the human race to colonise Mars.

Remind me again about how you can't "find the time" to achieve your goals?

I've got 24 hours. You've got 24 hours. We've *all* got 24 hours.

"We can't *find* the time. It's not lost. It's not missing. We haven't left it in the car or down the back of the sofa."

We have to *make* the time.

My business partner Jason took part in a charity challenge to raise money for Cancer Research UK. The challenge was to do 30 minutes of exercise every day throughout the month of September and to get people to sponsor you for doing so.

Cancer Research is a charity that is very close to Jason's heart. His family has been directly affected by that bastard of a disease and he's successfully raised more than £200,000 over the last few years as chairman of the local Relay for Life team.

Now, Jason's a busy man. As well as being chairman of that committee, he's also headed up the PTA at his children's school. He's got a wife, four children, one grandchild, two horses, a dog and four cats. His kids play football and hockey, so he's often playing "Dad's Cabs".

Oh, and he's a director of several companies, an angel investor, and mentor to more than 100 small businesses.

Jason hasn't got 30 minutes a day spare. Yet he "found" the time to complete the challenge.

Correction. He *made* the time to complete the challenge.

He blocked out the time in his diary every single day. And every single day, without fail, he did at least 30 minutes of exercise. He played golf, he played squash, and he tried roller skating, Zumba, circuit training, Rockfit, hip hop dancing, and Metafit. He even did some open-water swimming. In the sea. Without a wetsuit.

He still did it when he didn't feel like it. Even when it was pouring with rain. When he "didn't have time".

He made the time, every day. And that created a routine. A habit that stuck. Forcing himself to do the same thing for 30 minutes every day for a whole month gave Jason the momentum to carry on that routine into October and beyond. He's eased off from 30 minutes every day now, but the routine of getting regular exercise has been established.

Remember, too, that Jason created this new routine from a standing start. He did no dedicated exercise whatsoever in August, July or June.

But he got the bug. He established the routine. The first few days were tough. He was in a lot of pain after that first week, as he'd used muscles that hadn't been touched in years. He was battered, bruised and physically drained.

And then it got easier. He started to enjoy it. He posted selfies and videos on Facebook every time he did an activity – a new routine that provided him with accountability to ensure he followed through with the challenge, but one that also inspired others to be more active too.

There's always a delay between starting a new routine and seeing the results. After a week, Jason was a few pounds lighter and had raised around £50 for charity. Hardly worth it for all the effort he'd put in, right?

But by the end of the month, he'd lost a stone and a half in weight (around 20lbs) and raised almost £1,000 for Cancer Research UK. Not from a big one-off event, but from a 30-minute, daily routine. Day after day after day. Drip, drip, drip.

Jason didn't have the time to do it.

He didn't "find" the time.

He made the time.

If you say yes to this...

That's great. So how do I make time? Do I invent that 25th hour or add a 32nd day to January and March? Perhaps make every year a leap year and devise my very own calendar?

No, the easiest way to make time for what you want to do is to stop doing other things.

Remember the jar full of stones, pebbles, sand and water? You have to put the stones in first. And if there's no room left for pebbles, then you don't add any pebbles! Too many people fill their jars up with sand and water, and then complain that there's no room for the stones or pebbles.

You have to put the immovable objects in first.

Make time for working on the business. Make time for your health. Make time for your family and your relationships. Make time for your mindset and wellbeing. Make time for yourself. Make time for what's important to you.

Make that time.

Then and only then can you start adding the pebbles. And if there's time left in your day or your week, you can add some sand too. And maybe a little water.

But make the time for the important stuff first. Carve that time out in advance and protect it with your life.

Many people tell me that they "haven't got time" to work on their business and I've noticed weird phenomena about these people.

When I look at their Facebook feeds, they seem to "find" time every day to post on there and to like and comment on other's posts. Their own posts tend to talk about what TV programmes they've "found the time" to watch or which celebrity scandal they've "found the time" to read up about.

When I send them an email, they "find the time" to reply almost instantly. If I call them, they always "find the time" to answer.

They can tell you exactly what happened in Emmerdale last night, who left Strictly last week and who they want to win The X Factor this year. But ask them to spend 30 minutes a day working on their business or send out a weekly email? No, they "haven't got time" for that.

Conversely, some of our One Percenters are busy working *on* their business and they've also found that they're insanely busy, almost to breaking point.

They're not wasting hours every day watching Netflix or playing computer games. They're working their arses off. And to the untrained eye, they appear to be working on the right things – everything they're doing would appear to be moving the needle in the right direction.

The problem lies with their capacity.

We all have limits to how much we can do in a day. We all only have those 24 hours available to us. So why can Sir Richard Branson achieve so much more than me in 24 hours? It's because he has a lot more capacity. He's got huge systems and processes set up, tweaked and modified to run in the most efficient manner. He's got layer upon layer of staff, all highly trained and insanely capable. His management teams are literally the best in the business.

If Sir Richard Branson wants to start a new business tomorrow, all he needs to do is call one person from his team, ask them to set everything up and let him know where and when to turn up for the press launch.

You won't find Sir Richard answering emails at Virgin Media or ordering fuel for his planes. He doesn't do inductions at Virgin Active gyms or arrange overdrafts for Virgin Money customers. He doesn't devise the timetable for Virgin Trains and he certainly isn't stomping on grapes to make Virgin Wines (unless it's for a PR stunt of course).

Sir Richard is able to "juggle" so many different businesses in completely different sectors because he has the capacity and the structure to do so in a way that means he's never actually "juggling" anything. He has one role and that is to be the figurehead of the huge machine he's built over the last 50 years.

A common mistake I see small business owners make, especially those with a "Type A" personality, is to think that they need to grab every single opportunity that comes their way.

It's how you get started. You'll say yes to every job.

"Can you do x, y or z?" they ask.

"Yes, of course we can!" you answer. Then you figure out how the hell you're going to do it.

Ready, fire, aim! Start now, get perfect later. Good is good enough. Imperfect action trumps perfect inaction.

But if you say yes to every single opportunity that comes your way without focusing on increasing your capacity then you're going to reach your limit sooner rather than later. You'll hit the glass ceiling and start getting overwhelmed and stressed.

When I'm coaching one of our One Percenters and they come to me with a potential opportunity that they're considering, I'll probe what their current capacity looks like. How easily could they fit this new opportunity into their existing machine?

Will adding the extra work break things? What new systems, processes, staff members or physical items would need to be put in place to successfully integrate this new idea? And what about the business owner's headspace?

When just one week earlier they had told me they were maxed out working on Project X or that they had found themselves working evenings and weekends more frequently, I know that I need to question their capacity.

So I'll ask the following question: "If you say yes to this, what are you going to say no to?"

Because if you're at capacity and you add something new, something else has to give.

Very wet feet

I don't remember much from school, but I do remember learning about that Archimedes bloke getting in a bath full of water, noticing the bathroom floor was now flooded and yelling "Eureka!" I recall replicating his theory of displacement with measuring jugs full of water in our physics lessons.

You can try this one yourself in the relative safety of your own kitchen. Fill a jug right to the top with water and drop in an apple. Hey presto! Water all over the place. Eureka indeed.

This is what so many small business owners do. Their metaphorical jugs are already full to the brim, yet they're going around looking for new apples to chuck in. There's only one way that's going to end and it's going to be messy.

If your capacity is at or near the limit and an opportunity presents itself (as it inevitably will), you can do one of two things:

1. Get a bigger jug/increase your capacity.
2. Accept there needs to be some displacement/something's gotta give.

If you say yes to this, what are you going to say no to? If you say yes to this, are you saying no to spending time with your family? If you say yes to this, are you saying no to doing your own admin? If you say yes to this, are you saying no to taking a dividend this year? If you say yes to this, are you saying no to working with problem clients? If you say yes to this, are you saying no to a hobby? If you say yes to this, are you saying no to a less profitable part of the business? If you say yes to this, are you saying no to looking after your health?

If you say yes to a new routine, what routine(s) are you saying no to?

If you're at capacity and add something new, there will be displacement. You can choose either what gets displaced and remove it first or you can have very wet feet.

It's your choice.

Four candles and two levers

Jason and I are like yin and yang. We're two sides of the same coin. We think and work very differently. And that's why we work together so well – we complement each other. He's good at the things I suck at and I can do the things he can't.

Jason's superpower lies in operations, whereas mine is in marketing.

Jason's job is to set up nice, robust systems and processes that run the businesses on autopilot. Processes that can handle the entire customer journey. Systems that can take care of fulfilment. That require as little human input on a daily basis as possible and can be automated. That ensure we can sleep at night, knowing our businesses are in safe hands with Jason's systems and processes all working efficiently and effectively.

My job is to try to break those systems and processes by throwing loads of customers at them.

Think of your business as a big old clunky machine. There are two levers to change how it works. The first lever is the Operations Lever. This controls your capacity to cope with the level of business you currently get. Pushing this lever equals hiring new members of staff, putting automated systems and processes in place, and making the entire machine work more efficiently.

If you've got smoke coming out of the top of the machine right now and it's making a rather nasty clunking noise, that's a good sign that you probably need to adjust the Ops Lever.

The second lever is the Marketing Lever. This acts as an accelerator and gets more customers flowing through the machine, resulting in more profit being spewed out of the other end. If your machine is purring along silently, but hardly popping any gold coins out of the bottom of it, it may be time to step on the gas a little bit and push the Marketing Lever.

In our businesses, Jason is the only qualified operative of the Ops Lever and I'm fully trained in how to work the Marketing Lever. We both know exactly how far to push each lever and what will happen when we move them one notch or five notches, as well as how to spot when it's time to push our respective lever and when it's time to pull it back.

One of our recent angel investments was to buy into Three Sixty Mortgages, a mortgage broker specialising in buy-to-let mortgages for property investors.

The MD of the company, David, had set up the business on his own as a self-employed broker. Over the next few years, he said "yes" to every opportunity that came his way. He found himself speaking on stages, being interviewed on podcasts, winning awards, being featured in the Press and, of course, helping hundreds and hundreds of property investors get better deals on their mortgages.

He also found himself working 70 hours a week, often leaving the office at 11pm and getting home to find his young kids had already gone to bed. Never mind burning the candle at both ends, he was burning four candles at both ends. His health suffered and he knew something had to change. He knew he needed help, but he couldn't afford to step off the treadmill. He was already working 70 hours a week, so how could he possibly find the time to recruit someone else, train them up and show them the ropes?

He hadn't got the time to perfect all his systems and processes. He was too busy doing the doing. He hadn't got time to do any marketing either, which is just as well because he physically couldn't cope with any more business.

He was truly at capacity.

Enter John and Jason. As well as running our own businesses and coaching hundreds of small business owners through our One Percent Club, we're also angel investors.

Angel investment is a bit like you see on Dragons' Den (or Shark Tank for our American cousins), but we're much friendlier and less up our own arses than the Dragons.

We invested some money and, more importantly, time into Three Sixty Mortgages. We sat down with David and talked about what the business needed to thrive. And what it was crying out for was for someone to ratchet up the Operations Lever a good few notches.

Let's not break David, shall we?

At this point, David was doing everything. He'd answer the phone, go to the bank, stand at the photocopier for hours every week, meet with clients, talk to the lenders and pop into Staples for the office supplies. He had next to no automated systems and processes.

This is like shooting fish in a barrel for Jason. Even I could see David's machine shuddering and clunking, thick black smoke pouring out of it, and having to shout to make ourselves heard over the racket.

Jason simply rolled up his sleeves, cracked his knuckles and grabbed hold of the Ops Lever.

One notch: We get someone in part-time to do some admin immediately. The noise dampens down slightly.

Two notches: We find Tom, another experienced broker, and persuade him to come aboard as a director. The black smoke vanishes.

Three notches: We find a new CRM system that will automate a lot of the legwork David is currently doing. The machine stops shuddering.

We push the Ops Lever a touch more – half a notch at a time now – and lay the foundations for automated marketing systems, advertise for a full-time admin and work on improving David's routine.

By this stage, we're almost ready for me to come in and start easing up the Marketing Lever.

You've no idea how tough this has been for me. All I want to do in every business I'm involved in is to ramp up that Marketing Lever as far as it'll go.

Gary Halbert said: "There is no business problem, or any problem for that matter, that cannot be solved with a great sales letter."

That's a philosophy I fully buy into. Left to my own devices, I'd go full on Jeremy Clarkson-mode with the Marketing Lever: "POWER!!!"

But if I'd done that with Three Sixty Mortgages, I'd have broken the machine. It was already at breaking point. And never mind the machine; I'd have probably broken David, too.

I had to sit on my hands for months, itching to just ease that lever forward a touch. Maybe just half a notch? But I couldn't. The laws of displacement mean that if I did that, we'd all have wet feet and we'd need a new machine.

So I had to sit and watch Jason get the machine under control with the Ops Lever. Once it had stopped smoking and we could hear ourselves think, then I could start to plan how we were going to push the Marketing Lever up a notch or two.

Automated marketing systems were the first notch we moved to. We knew we could put these in place without putting any stress on the machine. Email follow-ups, testimonial requests, asking for referrals, chasing up leads, etc.

Then we put together a quarterly newsletter to go out to clients, letting them know about new products, changes to the law, how we can restructure their portfolio and case studies showing how much money Three Sixty Mortgages saved other clients.

The machine was still humming nicely. This is good.

Next, we started work on the social media strategy; easing it in gently. This is a half-notch turn. We weren't spending £2k a day on Facebook Ads yet. We wanted to see how the machine reacts to a few posts a week.

Brrrr! Whrrr! That's OK.

"I've arranged for you to have lunch with the business editor of the local paper." There's a little heat coming off the machine now.

"How about we do a re-launch event? We'll hire the ballroom of a hotel, invite all of our clients and the Press, have a load of guest speakers and cake for everyone, that sort of thing?"

Bang!

Ooh, that didn't sound good. It might be time to pull the Marketing Lever back a notch, just till we can ratchet up the Ops Lever a tad more and get the machine running smoothly again.

How is *your* machine running right now? Does it need some WD40 and a 32mm spanner or is it ready for the scrapheap? Which lever do you need to move? And do you have a qualified person to operate each lever?

Homework

Task: Say no to three different people in the next 24 hours. Practice asking yourself: "If I say yes to this, what am I saying no to?"

11. BORING, BORING, ARSENAL

Anyone who watched football back in the early 90s will be aware of the terrace chant "boring, boring Arsenal", which was aimed at George Graham's title-winning side of the time.

The Gunners had a tendency to edge out a lot of teams by a single goal. Arsenal 1, Opponents 0 was a regular result on the Grandstand vidiprinter each Saturday afternoon. In 1991, they won their tenth league title - their second in three years - finishing nine points above Liverpool.

For me, the standout statistic from the final league table is how few goals the Gunners conceded in that year. Eighteen in 38 matches – that's one goal every 2.11 games. Their closest rivals Liverpool let in 40 – more than one goal in every game.

Graham's team won the league twice in three years, just by being consistent. Their defence was legendary. As former manager Arsene Wenger commented: "When I first came to Arsenal, I realised the back four were all university graduates in the art of defending. As for Tony Adams, I consider him to be a doctor of defence."

The Arsenal back four was so widely respected that it was even referenced in the 1997 film The Full Monty, which was about a group of unemployed steelworkers from Sheffield who become male strippers to make ends meet.

In one scene, they're trying to synchronise a particular move and the actor Paul Barber (better known as Denzil in Only Fools and Horses) utters the line: "It's the Arsenal offside trap, isn't it? Whenever any bugger looks like scoring, we all step forward in a line and wave our arms about like a fairy."

That's how effective "boring" Arsenal were. Boring enough that they won title after title. Boring enough that they were immortalised in a blockbuster movie years later. Boring enough that they're still remembered as legends to this day.

That team didn't yet have flair players like Ian Wright, Dennis Bergkamp or Thierry Henry. It had a unit – the Arsenal back four – who did the right thing every time. They took no risks. They did nothing fancy. They avoided unforced errors, which frustrated their opponents and caused *them* to take more risks, make unforced errors and end up losing the game.

Usually 1-0 to the Arsenal.

Meanwhile in a parallel universe

While boring, boring Arsenal were off winning their boring, boring titles, fans of Plymouth Argyle were treated to something similar – former player David Kemp was just about keeping us in the old Second Division (which is now known as the Championship). With no money to spend whatsoever and the club located in the deep South West of the country, it was hard to attract quality players and so Kemp also deployed a "safety-first" strategy.

Unfortunately, Plymouth Argyle didn't have the luxury of being able to call on Tony Adams, Lee Dixon, Steve Bould or Nigel Winterburn, so most of their games ended up Plymouth 0, Opponents 1. And Argyle ended up sliding to the bottom of the table at the start of 1992.

Chairman Dan McCauley wanted a safe pair of hands to steer the Pilgrims to safety. And, naturally, the safest pair of hands he could think of was former England goalkeeper (and victim of the Hand of God) Peter Shilton.

It didn't work. Argyle were relegated that year.

But Mr McCauley stuck with Shilton and opened up his chequebook, allowing him to spend money and rebuild the team with flair and attacking football at its core.

In came players like Steve Castle, Paul Dalton, Dwight Marshall, Kevin Nugent, Steve McCall and Alan Nicholls, and a style of football never seen before (or since) at Home Park.

In the 1993/94 season, Plymouth Argyle outscored every other team in the country. Nobody scored more goals than the Green Army. They bagged 88 league goals – including an 8-1 thrashing of Hartlepool on the final day of the season.

And they finished third. In the third tier of English football. Only the top two get automatic promotion to the Championship.

Argyle ended up in the play-offs where they lost to Burnley in the semi-finals.

Then it all fell apart the following season. Record signing Peter Swan hated every moment of playing for the club. Key players got injured. Shilton fell out with McCauley and was sacked. The chequebook was slammed shut and Argyle found themselves relegated to the fourth tier for the first time in their history.

They've now been back there three times since.

Argyle of 1993 were exciting to watch, but they ultimately achieved nothing and crashed and burned.

Arsenal of 1991 were boring, but they were effective. They wanted to win the league, and they did.

Staring at a wall = gold medals

Routines are boring though, aren't they? Doing the same old thing every single day, day after day after day, week after week, month after month, and year after year?

Yep. Routines *are* boring. They're not sexy. They're not exciting.

Tony Adams & Co working every single day on perfecting the timing for their offside trap? Boring as hell, I'd imagine. Every young footballer dreams of scoring a wonder goal – a bicycle kick in the FA Cup Final or the free kick that takes you to the World Cup. But the reality for most footballers is hours and hours of learning to track back, keep your shape and do your job.

Routine is boring because it's every day. It's just the norm. You don't have to think about it. You can perform on autopilot.

And that's the point.

Remember how Warren Buffett and Charlie Munger turned ten grand into £240million? By being "consistently not stupid". By not making unforced errors. They look for the boring. They spend their days hunting for the mundane. Looking for safe, humdrum slam-dunks that they know they can plug into their existing machine, know how it works and know what results to expect.

Would you rather be bored or overwhelmed? Cartoonist Cathy Thorne jokes: "I love routine. Until I'm bored. Then I love excitement. Until I'm overwhelmed. Then I love routine."

If you want to succeed and improve your life, you have to embrace and fall in love with boredom. If you only do the work when it excites you and only put the hours in when it's convenient to do so, you'll never be consistent enough to make that breakthrough.

On Christmas Eve 2007, Royal Marines Commando Mark Ormrod was performing a routine foot patrol in the Helmand Province of Afghanistan when he stepped on an improvised explosive device.

An innovative and dangerous procedure carried out on board a Chinook helicopter en route to an emergency field hospital saved his life. Mark woke up three days later in Selly Oak Hospital, Birmingham. Both of his legs had been amputated above the knee and his right arm had been amputated above the elbow. He was the UK's first triple amputee to survive the Afghanistan conflict.

During his recovery, the doctors told Mark that he'd never walk again and that he should prepare himself for the rest of his life in a wheelchair.

But Mark has not used a wheelchair since June 2009. Not only does he now walk, but he also runs, cycles, swims and rows – not just for leisure, but at a competitive level.

Mark has competed in the Invictus Games, an international adaptive multi-sport event created by Prince Harry in which wounded, injured or sick armed services personnel and veterans take part in competitive sports.

When Mark was training for the games in Australia in 2018, he said the hardest part wasn't learning how to use the indoor rowing machine with his artificial limbs, working through the pain barrier or building up his endurance, stamina or speed. No, hitting the wall wasn't the problem – it was staring at the wall.

When you look at the video of Mark competing in Invictus, you see a stadium full of tens of thousands of people. You also imagine the audience of millions watching on TV.

But what you don't see is Mark, alone in his home gym, sitting on the rowing machine and looking at a blank wall.

Rowing.

For 90 minutes at a time.

Rowing.

Staring at that blank wall, rowing backwards and forwards, forwards and backwards. Time and time again. Just repeating the same action, looking at the same wall.

Every day for almost a year.

Mark won gold medals in both the Men's Four-Minute Endurance and the Men's One-Minute Sprint races. Technically, he won them in Australia.

But you and I know they were actually won in Mark's home gym during those hundreds of hours spent looking at a blank wall.

Mark Ormrod is a Routine Machine.

It would have been easy for Mark to quit. He could have made any number of excuses about the pain, the time commitment or simply the sheer inconvenience of training for a competitive event like Invictus.

What was most likely to cause him to fail, though, was boredom.

When training is boring, it's easy to skip a session or two. And once you've skipped one or two, it's easy to skip a bunch more. And once you've skipped that many, well, you'd just as well give up and do something interesting instead!

I can guarantee you that for almost any new routine you implement, there will be days where you feel like quitting. And the biggest threat to your continued implementation will be boredom.

But when you embrace the boredom, you achieve consistency. And when you're consistent over a prolonged period of time, that's when you start seeing truly remarkable results.

Baa Humbug!

I hate Christmas. OK, so I said earlier that I enjoyed the food. But for the King of Routine, Christmas is a nightmare. Go ahead – call me Scrooge or call me the Grinch, but it's true.

Every single one of your usual routines is kicked to the curb. You don't know what day of the week it is. Mince pies and a glass of Baileys are deemed acceptable for breakfast. You have to stay up three hours past your usual bedtime because it's New Year's Eve. The gym is closed for a whole day and a half and the entire world shuts down.

Roy Wood may have sung about "wishing it was Christmas every day", but would he *really* like to spend every day driving around Tesco car park for half an hour just to try to find a space? Would he really want to never work again? To be honest, the estimated £180,000 cheque for royalties that has dropped on his doormat every year since 1973 means he probably doesn't need to.

Of course, I have Christmas routines. You'd expect nothing less from me, I'm sure. My main task for the big day is to cook the lunch, which last year was turkey and all the trimmings for 12 people. Preparing all that may sound hard, but it's actually dead easy. I simply dust off my routine from the previous year.

The gammon gets cooked on Christmas Eve and all sliced up. The veg is all peeled, prepped and chopped. The turkey goes in the oven at 7.30am on Christmas Day, a festive playlist goes on, and I spend the next hour or two watching the kids open their presents, hunting for batteries and assembling various toys. By 11am, the turkey is done and can rest, and then the fun really starts.

Over the next two hours, I follow a simple timeline that has served me well for many years. Stuffing is prepared. Potatoes are roasted. Parsnips and carrots are drizzled in honey and whacked in the oven. Pigs in blankets are fried and rested. Sausage meat is roasted. Brussels sprouts and broccoli are boiled. Gravy is simmering. And the Christmas pudding is steaming away in the slow cooker.

Every now and then someone will pop into the kitchen and ask if there's anything they can do. The answer is always "no" because although it looks like I'm juggling 15 different things at once, the routine – the structure of what to do and when to do it – is taking all the strain.

It's the routine that does all the work. I'm just the sous chef following the plan.

Each year, I'll tweak the routine to improve things. I'll reduce the time the turkey's in the oven so that it doesn't dry out. I'll try out Jamie Oliver's recipe for wok-fried sprouts. I'll use a meat slicing machine to get nice, uniform, thin slices of meat that can be easily stored in the fridge for the next week.

My key takeaway from my Christmas lunch debrief last year was not to buy so much food this year (it turns out that 10kg of meat is *way* too much for 12 people). There's only so much turkey curry and gammon and eggs that you can stomach.

Every time I iterate the Christmas lunch routine, I make things a little bit better. A touch easier. A tad less stressful. This means I can actually enjoy the day rather than fretting over whether the potatoes are done or whether we're going to give anyone food poisoning from under-cooked turkey.

Don't get me wrong: I don't actually hate Christmas. I love the *idea* of Christmas. I go all out to ensure that my kids enjoy the magic of the festive period. I'll pull a cracker and pig out on turkey and Christmas pudding like everyone else.

But after more than a few days of having to ask Alexa what day it is and eating Christmas cake for breakfast, I start to get cravings.

Cravings for salad.

Cravings for exercise.

Cravings to do some work.

More than anything else, I'm craving routine.

My favourite day of the Christmas holiday is the second of January. It's the day that the Christmas tree comes down, the junk food gets locked away or thrown out, and I can go to the gym, eat a nice big salad and get some productive work done.

My second favourite day of the holiday is the day that the kids go back to school. Again, don't get me wrong. I love my family. Spending quality time with them is the reason why I do what I do. For me, it's all about getting the work/life balance right. And having spent the last two weeks almost completely at the "life" end of the see-saw, it's time to get some balance again.

I love my boys being home and the house full of joy and laughter. But they're also brothers who are two years apart, so as well as joy and laughter, the house also sees its fair share of tantrums, fights and arguments.

And for someone who craves routine, walking into the house after dropping the boys at school that first morning in January and being greeted with silence? Pure bliss. It's great to be back. The King of Routine has returned to his throne.

Six hours of uninterrupted productive work follow (broken only by a nice healthy lunch) and then it's time to pick the boys up from school again. By which point, I've really missed having them around. And having spent six hours back at the "work" end of the see-saw, I'm ready for some fun time with my boys.

Now, where did I put the Quality Street?

What's the best piece of marketing you've ever done?

We have an on-boarding questionnaire for people who join our One Percent Club. It helps us find out a little about both the business and the person behind the business. We get to find out what makes you tick and what's holding you back.

One of the questions we ask all new One Percenters is: "What's the best piece of marketing you've ever done?" And it's really interesting to see different people's responses to this question.

They tend to range from, "I haven't done any marketing" or "I use word of mouth" (which, by the way, is the same thing as "I haven't done any marketing"), up to "I sent this leaflet out" or "We had a Black Friday sale".

And then I'll get some really interesting ones.

"I spoke on stage at an event three years ago."

"I sent a sales letter to 30 of my ideal clients a while back."

"I was in the paper once."

When I get one of these people on a coaching call, I like to grill them a little bit on that marketing that they told me was the best they'd ever done.

"So you spoke on stage three years ago?"

"Yes, it was really scary. But well worth it. I got 13 new clients as a result."

"Wow, that's great! And how much is that worth to you?"

"I charge £2,000 a head, plus some ongoing. So at least £26,000. But it's probably double that with the ongoing."

"So about £50,000? How long were you on stage for?"

"About 25 minutes."

"And how long did it take you to prep for it?"

"About two days."

"OK, so £50,000 for two days prep and 25 minutes work?"

"Haha, yep. When you put it like that..."

"So why haven't you done it again in the last three years?"

Eventually, we discover the reason he hadn't repeated "the most successful piece of marketing he'd ever done" was because no one had asked him to. He did the live event in the first place because he was asked to and he said "yes".

He never thought he could actually go out and offer his services to event organisers. He'd already done the prep, so all he'd have to do is deliver the content. Twenty-five minutes work for £50k.

He's got capacity to take on another 30 clients every year, so he only needs to find two live events per year to achieve this and bring in a brand new £100,000 a year revenue stream.

When you've got marketing that works, you need to turn it into marketing that works *routinely.*

In '*Big Ideas... for Small Businesses*', I detailed the best marketing campaign that I'd ever done. It was one that we originally ran for our sports betting business back in 2016 and it brought in a decent six-figure sum in four short weeks.

I walked through all the individual components of the campaign and looked at what worked, what we could improve and why it worked so well. I laid out the template right there for you to swipe and deploy if you so wanted.

And because it is the best piece of marketing I've ever done for *that* business, I've repeated it. I ran the same campaign (albeit tweaked and improved) in 2017, then 2018 and again in 2019 – and plan to do so in 2020. I've adapted it and taken it into other sectors and other businesses in which I'm involved. I've broken it down into its individual elements and borrowed parts of it for other campaigns.

When you've got marketing that works, you need to turn it into marketing that works *routinely.*

Incidentally, my first book was the best piece of marketing I've done for the One Percent Club. That's why I'm writing another one. When you've got marketing that works, you need to turn it into marketing that works *routinely.*

But that's too easy?

"There must be more to it than that," I hear you cry. "It's got to be more complicated!"

Nope. Putting a new routine in place is easy to do. But then it's just as easy to not do it too.

Too often we look for the complex rather than accepting the simple. We over-analyse the micro and forget to look at the macro. We'd rather find the "weird trick" diet that involves eating nothing but bananas all day and downing a pint of apple cider vinegar before bed (that's not a real diet as far as I'm aware – but if anyone tries it and it works, remember I own the patent, alright?), rather than adjust your macros and get in a caloric deficit.

We'd rather believe that there's some "secret" to business success that we're missing out on, rather than offering products and services that people want and asking those people to buy.

The path to wealth must lie with choosing the right stock, having the right day-trading strategy or picking the right cryptocurrency, right? It's got nothing to do with pound cost averaging and compounding over the long term.

Stop looking for the cheats, hacks, shortcuts and "get rich quick" schemes. Start looking for the slow and steady. The tortoise rather than the hare. Get rich slowly.

Take the boring, easy, slow path to success. It'll take you a while to get there, but you will get there if you just keep heading in the right direction and keep putting one foot in front of the other.

Homework

Question: Do you want to be Plymouth Argyle and outscore every other team or would you rather win the league?

12. THIS SHIT TAKES TIME

What do you see when you look at successful people? Wealth? Fame? Glamour? Respect? The billionaire hopping on his private jet after meeting with the Prime Minister?

The Olympian on the winning podium, chest puffed out, beaming with pride while the national anthem plays and a gold medal draped around her neck?

The lead singer of the band milking the adoration of the crowd after their Glastonbury headline set?

That's the tip of the iceberg you're looking at. You're seeing the tiny bit of the story that is currently visible. You're not seeing what's gone before.

You're not seeing the billionaire eating beans on toast in his bedsit 20 years earlier as he tried (and failed) to get a meeting with the regional purchasing manager of a small chain of restaurants. You don't see him maxing out his credit cards and working 100-hour weeks just to survive. You don't see him lose everything and go bankrupt. Twice. You've no idea how close he came to giving up.

You don't see the Olympian at school being told that she "wasn't cut out for PE". You don't see her getting up at 4am on a freezing Tuesday morning in February to fit in three hours of training before going to work. You don't see her apologising for the umpteenth time to her friends, explaining that she can't go out drinking with them this weekend as she's got a competition coming up in nine weeks' time. You don't see her throwing up into a bucket during training sessions because she's pushed herself beyond breaking point. You don't know how many times she's been told to "give up and get a real job".

You don't see the lead singer of the band playing to three men and a dog in a backstreet pub, barely earning enough money to cover the petrol for the dilapidated old van that they're humping their own equipment around in. You've no idea how many hours they've spent practicing in the garage to perfect their songs. You don't know how many times they were rejected by record label after record label. You can't remember a time when no radio station would play them.

When you see an iceberg, you're actually only seeing 8.3 per cent of the ice. The other 91.7 per cent of the iceberg is hidden underwater. But it's there. The visible part of the iceberg could not exist without it, but you can't see it. Out of sight, out of mind.

When people see success, they see the money, the fame, and the talent. They don't see the discipline, the failures, or the sacrifice. They don't see the persistence, the disappointments, the hard work, and the dedication.

They see the effect, but not the cause.

They try to replicate that success, based on the 8.3 per cent they can see. But they forget about the 91.7 per cent that went before – the foundations that made it all possible. The first big wave that comes along destroys their "iceberg", turning it into more of a Slush Puppy.

Bamboo lies dormant for the first five years of its life with no visible growth whatsoever above ground. Yet, as long as the farmer continues to cultivate it, the grass will build up a powerful network of roots, a strong foundation under the soil. But the farmer still has no visible results from his half a decade of labour.

Suddenly, six weeks later, the bamboo is 90 feet tall. The work happened over the five years, not the six weeks. As Warren Buffet noted:

> *"Someone's sitting in the shade today because someone planted a tree a long time ago."*

Duct tape not required

Do you want your child to win Wimbledon in 20 years' time? Here's a proven model for success. Take your average three-year-old, duct-tape tennis rackets to their arms (they aren't strong enough to hold them properly yet and you don't want them to be able to let go), and fire 2,500 tennis balls a day at them.

Repeat this for 20 years (you can probably remove the duct tape after a year or two).

That may not sound like the best modern parenting advice, but that's exactly how 1992 Wimbledon champion Andre Agassi learned how to play tennis. Agassi describes in his excellent 2009 autobiography *'Open'* how his father, a professional boxer, forced him into playing tennis against his will – including the duct tape method.

Andre tells us that Agassi Snr believed in the 10,000-hour rule – that if any child played enough tennis, he could be a world champion. "My father says that if I hit 2,500 balls each day, I'll hit 17,500 balls each week, and at the end of one year I'll have hit nearly one million balls. He believes in math. Numbers, he says, don't lie. A child who hits one million balls each year will be unbeatable."

There was just one small problem: Andre didn't like tennis.

He didn't enjoy hitting a million balls a year. He hated being sent away to a dedicated tennis academy. The duct tape might have been removed by now, but his father's unfaltering commitment to raising a world champion was more powerful than ever.

Every year, Andre would hit his million balls. He'd train every day and compete every weekend. And he got better.

He got good. Very good.

By the time he was 15, he was labelled a "natural" and was wiping the floor with most of the adults he was playing against. If only those commentators had seen the duct tape or the million balls a year or the four hours training every day. They might not have been so quick to call him a "natural".

After a few years on the professional circuit, Andre had risen almost to the top. But not quite. He got stuck. He couldn't seem to grind out "ugly" wins against stubborn, unadventurous opponents who rarely made a mistake.

And then he went for a beer with his friend Perry Rogers and Brad Gilbert, who was a big-time blackjack player in Las Vegas.

Gilbert told him: "It takes 21 sets to win a Grand Slam. That's all. You need to win just 21 sets. Seven matches, best of five. That's 21. In tennis, like cards, 21 is a winner. Blackjack!

"Focus on that number and you won't go wrong. Simplify, simplify. Every time you win a set, say to yourself 'That's one down. That's one in my pocket.' At the start of a tournament, count backward from 21. When I'm playing blackjack, I'd rather win with 16, because that's winning ugly. There's no need to win with 21. No need to be perfect."

Agassi then went on a massive losing streak. He said that trying to undo the "showman" in him and play the simple "ugly 21" strategy that Gilbert advised was like "trying to play left-handed" for weeks and weeks.

And then it clicked. Sure enough, Agassi started being able to grind out those ugly wins. He may have stopped winning with a flourish or after tremendous rallies, but he'd get his 21 sets.

Those 21 sets became his new "million balls".

Just like Roald Amundson had his 15 miles a day, or Stephen King's ten pages a day, or Paul Bleck's one email a week, or the Arsenal back four's offside trap.

Simplify, simplify.

Win ugly.

And Agassi won plenty of course, including 76 per cent of his 1,144 matches, 60 career titles, eight Grand Slams, an Olympic gold medal and the adulation of millions.

Just keep the duct tape away from your children...

What doesn't kill you...

Smoking a cigarette probably won't kill you.

Smoking 20 cigarettes probably won't kill you.

Smoke 20 a day for 40 years, though, and there's a pretty good chance that it *will* kill you.

What you did yesterday doesn't matter. What you do today doesn't matter. What you do tomorrow doesn't matter.

What you do *every day* matters. What you do *routinely* matters.

Eating a salad for lunch today isn't going to make you thin. But replacing your normal burger and fries lunch with a healthy, nutritious salad every day will. If you keep packing on the right snowflakes and rolling it down the hill of time, you'll get there. Even if in the short term you don't see any visible progress.

It's ironic that all these things that create success in the long term don't actually appear to be making one iota of difference in the short term. By the time you get the feedback from the changes, you've already done the hard work and the new routine is ingrained.

Conversely, the routines and habits that cause damage and kill your hopes and dreams actually give you almost instant, positive feedback. Burgers and fries taste good. Milkshakes taste good. Skiving off work and playing video games feels good.

Good in the short term, bad in the long term.

My mouth tastes so bad all of a sudden

You may have heard of Pavlov's Dogs. Russian psychologist Ivan Pavlov conducted an experiment in which he was able to train dogs to salivate on command – specifically upon the ringing of a bell. This process became known as "classic conditioning" and is achieved by delivering a reward at the same time as a trigger.

Ring the bell, give a treat.

Ring the bell, give a treat.

Ring the bell, give a treat.

You get the idea.

Eventually, you can ring the bell and the dog will expect the treat, anticipate the reward, already taste the juicy goodness in their mouth and begin to salivate in readiness for the forthcoming feast – without actually getting the treat.

There was a great visual demonstration of this process in the US version of the TV show The Office. In one scene, Jim reboots his computer, which produces the classic Windows "ding dong" noise and he offers his colleague Dwight a mint.

Over the course of several weeks (via a 20-second montage), Jim is shown repeating this action and offering Dwight a mint every time he reboots his computer, just after the "ding dong" sound. The punchline to this scene occurs when Jim reboots his computer for the final time.

"Ding dong."

This time Jim doesn't offer a mint. But Dwight automatically puts his hand out to receive one.

"What are you doing, Dwight?"

Dwight looks confused and says he doesn't know. He then proceeds to salivate and announces to the camera: "My mouth tastes so bad all of a sudden."

Pavlov's dogs. Dwight Schrute. You. Me.

We all respond to feedback.

You may not get the instant feedback you'd like when changing your routines. Swapping out your burger for a salad isn't going to make those bingo wings disappear overnight. It will eventually, but why not cheat in the meantime?

By "cheat", I don't mean have the burger *and* the salad! I mean give yourself some artificial feedback until the real stuff shows up. Go without a cigarette today and you can watch your favourite film tonight. Write that sales letter now and go to your favourite restaurant for lunch. Eat healthily for a week and enjoy a "cheat" meal.

Ring your own damn bell.

Train yourself.

Take the right action. Ring the bell. Have a treat.

Take the right action. Ring the bell. Have a treat.

Take the right action. Ring the bell. Have a treat.

Take the right action. Salivate.

The Stay Puft Marshmallow Man

Walter Mischel, a psychology professor at Stanford University in California, performed a series of studies on more than 600 children in the late 1960s and early 1970s, which became known as the "marshmallow test". It was designed to study the impact of delayed gratification.

In the studies, each child was offered a choice. They could have one marshmallow right now or they could wait a few minutes and have two marshmallows.

Some of the children opted to have the solitary marshmallow immediately, while the vast majority of kids cottoned on quickly that two was a bigger number than one and that waiting a few minutes to have twice as many snacks was a pretty good idea.

The children were then left in the room for between ten and 15 minutes.

Alone.

With the marshmallow.

When the adults returned to the room, two-thirds of the children had eaten the marshmallow. Only one child in three was able to resist the temptation of immediate gratification and patiently wait for their second marshmallow.

For two-thirds of the children, their Monkey made their choice before their Human had a chance to pipe up. They made the emotional decision that "a bird in the hand is worth two in the bush", and popped the marshmallow into their mouths.

The kids who waited it out managed to let their Human make a logical decision. Two is indeed more than one.

Follow-up studies were performed on all 600-plus children. At regular intervals over the coming decades, every single child was measured for SAT scores, body mass index, average income, educational attainment and social standing.

The children who waited for the second marshmallow were more successful in every measure than those who snaffled the first one. They were healthier. They had better qualifications. They lived longer. They earned more. They lived in a better part of town. They drove better cars. They went on better holidays.

The children who were able to delay their gratification outperformed those who took instant gratification in every single measurement.

The routine of allowing the Human to make most of the decisions (including programming the Computer) rather than the Monkey, compounded over a few decades, enabled those kids to turn one marshmallow into something the size of the Stay Puft Marshmallow Man.

Instant gratification gives you instant feedback and instant rewards. Delayed gratification gives you delayed feedback and delayed rewards. But in the long run, those rewards taste so much sweeter than one lousy marshmallow.

Teaching an old dog new tricks

Chewie and I have been attending puppy class every week with a lovely lady called Cassie.

Cassie's got four dogs and a husband, so she's used to training animals. Her method is pretty simple – she uses positive reinforcement in the form of a clicker and some food (primarily for the dogs, but I'm sure it works on husbands too).

When your dog does something you want it to do, such as sit down, give you eye contact or lie on its bed, you reward immediately with a "click" of the clicker (a small plastic device that makes a clicking noise when you press a button) followed by a tasty treat.

It doesn't take the dogs long to cotton on to this feedback loop. Within 30 seconds, Chewie had figured out that if he gave me eye contact, he got a treat. If he sat on his bed, he got a treat.

"Click," followed by food. It's Pavlov's Dogs all over again.

If Chewie barks or jumps up at my leg, he gets ignored. No eye contact. No attention. No click and no treat. No feedback whatsoever.

The rules of this game are simple. Do the right things and you earn a reward, but do the wrong things and you get nothing.

The dogs naturally gravitate towards doing the right things. And so would you.

We all respond to feedback. We know that touching a hot frying pan will hurt, so we don't do it again. Eating a piece of chocolate tastes good, so we immediately want to have another one.

When I first started training Chewie, I was told not to give him any commands at all. I wasn't allowed to tell him what to do. He was a two-month-old puppy and doesn't understand English yet. He doesn't know what I mean when I say: "Get off the bloody sofa, for the last time, will you!"

I'm merely told to praise and reward him whenever he makes good decisions as part of his natural routine. In doing this, I'm actually helping to shape his future routine to be the kind of dog that I'd like to have.

Sit calmly and wait for food? Click.

Settle down on your bed? Click.

Greet visitors with all four paws on the ground? Click.

Go to the toilet out on the grass? Click.

You can do the same with almost any animal, including your children, husband, wife or even yourself. I'm not suggesting you buy a clicker for them. In my experience, spouses don't respond anywhere near as well as puppies to a bit of squeezy cheese, a pat on the head and a shout of, "Who's a good girl, then? You are! You are! Yes, you are!"

But if you want your teenager to keep their room tidy, then you might want to stop moaning and nagging at them for not keeping it tidy. You've been doing that for years now and it's not working. Instead, try dishing out some praise when they do something – *anything* – to keep it tidy.

If your daughter brings one cup downstairs after using it, praise her for doing so. "Thanks for doing that." When your son makes his bed, say: "Your bed looks nice like that."

If they tidy one small area of their room – say they clear a desk or tidy a shelf – say: "Wow, your room's looking really tidy. Well done!"

Be genuine with your praise. Don't lace it with sarcasm and certainly don't turn it into a shit sandwich like this: "Your room's looking nice at the moment. It's a shame you can't keep it like this all the time. Anyway, good job."

As the behaviour becomes more akin to the behaviour you'd like, you can start to add rewards as well as praise. Why not let them choose a new rug or some new bedding? Something that's going to reinforce the positive behaviour and get them to take pride in a nice, tidy bedroom.

Even though you know how this "trick" works, you can still use the same techniques on yourself.

Let's say you want to learn Spanish. Each time you display a behaviour that helps you move towards your goal, give yourself a mental "click" – some immediate feedback that you're doing the right thing. Want to watch your favourite film tonight? Why not watch it with Spanish subtitles on? Click. Have a bag of popcorn as a treat. Feedback.

You happen to bump into a Spanish speaker while on a night out and take the opportunity to test your ability to speak the lingo. Click. Have some sangria to celebrate. Feedback.

Switch your mobile phone's default language to Spanish. Click. And spend the next 20 minutes playing Pájaros Enojados. Feedback.

Every time you take the right actions, give immediate feedback and reward.

What gets rewarded gets repeated, whether we're talking about dogs, teenagers, husbands, employees – or you.

The world's worst harvest festival

It takes 21 days to build a habit. No, it doesn't, it takes 30 days. Sorry, I mean 60 days. Or is it 90?

The actual answer is – it depends.

Sorry.

The length of time it takes for a new routine to become a fully-established, automatic habit depends entirely on each individual case. There are so many variables at play here:

- How ingrained your current routines are.
- How badly you desire a different outcome.
- How hard the new routine is.
- How quickly you'll see results from the new routine.

Can you imagine going to a farmers' market and learning that all the different fruit and vegetables grew at exactly the same rate?

"It takes 21 days to grow a vegetable," announces the farmer. "It doesn't matter if it's Brussels sprouts or a pumpkin. Soil conditions, rainfall, fertiliser and temperature all count for nothing. It takes 21 days, no matter what."

That sounds ridiculous, doesn't it? And clearly wrong. Yet people still buy into this 21 day BS when it comes to routines.

When growing vegetables, you understand that you need to plant the seeds, cultivate the young veg and harvest them only when the vegetables are fully-grown. You can't just chuck some seeds in the ground, wander back three weeks later and dig up whatever's there. That would be the world's worst harvest festival.

It doesn't matter how long it takes. What matters is that it *does* happen. If the Human repeats a task manually enough times then the Computer will write a program to automate it. The key is not to worry about how many days you need to manually override the Computer, but rather to put systems, tools and technology in place to help that happen.

Whether that's a sticker chart, reminders and apps on your phone, visual clues or attaching the new routine to an existing one, anything that you can do to ensure compliance by the Human just long enough for the Computer to take over and write the script will help.

(Whilst 30 days isn't a one-size-fits-all magic number, it's long enough to give you some serious momentum, and deal with the early wobbles when establishing a new routine. That's why I created a free 30-day challenge for readers of this book - you'll find details at the end of the book.)

The feedback loop is the biggest factor in the length of time taken for the Computer to take over. When a child touches a hot stove, they learn very quickly that touching hot things with bare skin is not a great behaviour to repeat.

But cleaning teeth? That might take a few Human parents nagging, coercing, bribing, threatening and modelling before the child's Computer is programmed to do it twice a day on autopilot. And I say that as the parent of two young boys, who twice a day respond to my question of whether they have brushed their teeth with the exact same answer: "Oh, I forgot!"

Mr Bull knows the answer

I've done a lot to dampen your spirits in this chapter. I've warned you that achieving the huge levels of success that you see displayed publicly will take years and years of hard work, determination and perseverance.

I've told you that things are going to be tough, that you need to work consistently for long periods of time without getting any positive feedback whatsoever, and that life's going to throw you curveballs and knock you off your perch just when you think you're almost at the summit.

That's all true.

If you're looking for instant success or the latest get rich quick scheme, then pop that solitary marshmallow into your mouth and I'll wish you all the best.

For the rest of us, becoming a Routine Machine is a proven path to success. But it's a long, winding path and there are no shortcuts. There are signposts along the way, though, to show you that you're still heading in the right direction and it's these signposts that you should train yourself to look out for.

Have you ever been on a car journey with children? If so, then you've probably heard the immortal words, "Are we there yet?" more than a few times. I know I have. Usually every 15 minutes until we eventually do arrive at our destination.

Children ask this out of natural curiosity. We all want to know what to expect. What time will we be there? How much longer are we going to be in the car? What should I do to pass the time?

My default answer when the kids ask how long something's going to take is borrowed from one of their own personal heroes – Mr Bull from Peppa Pig.

What's Mr Bull's answer when he's asked how long the road to the park will be closed? "It will take... as long as it will take."

Absolutely, 100 per cent true. Not very helpful, admittedly, but completely true.

So how long will it take for you to "get there" in your quest for success? It will take... as long as it will take.

But it won't take that long to start seeing signs that good things are coming. Just as you start to notice the daffodils poking their green shoots out of the ground in the middle of winter, you will start to notice positive feedback from your new routines.

And, as you know, once you start getting the feedback, the hard work is already done. That 91.7 per cent of the iceberg is underwater and most of the daffodil is still underground at this point. Train yourself to spot the feedback and use it to keep you on track.

When I started my fruit and vegetable juicing routine, I saw no feedback at all for the first few days. I didn't particularly enjoy the taste of a green juice and would much rather have been enjoying a carbolicious lunch. But I persevered and after a week or so, I started receiving some feedback. I was a few pounds lower on the scales and I was noticeably sleeping better at night.

Nothing earth-shattering, but it gave me just enough feedback to keep me going. A signpost that I was on the right path and I knew that all I had to do was keep putting one foot in front of the other.

Two weeks in and I was half a stone lighter. I'd dropped a jean size. I had more energy.

More signposts.

After a month of the new routine, I'd gone down another jean size and now noticed improvements to my skin, nails and hair. My eyes looked brighter. I found clarity in my thinking and decision-making that simply wasn't there before.

Even more signposts.

Six months later and that one routine had changed my life. The feedback started coming within a few days and I kept noticing more and more signposts coming as I stayed on the path.

Feedback is fuel. Use it to keep you on track. Whatever your goal is, it might take you a month to achieve or it might take you ten years. But train yourself to spot the signposts – they'll keep you on the right path.

The "secret" to becoming a Routine Machine is knowing you're doing the right things. Even when you don't get instant feedback or instant gratification, you know that as long as you keep doing what you're doing you will get the results. Just keep on the path and keep following the signposts.

It will take as long as it will take. But you know – you just *know* – that if you keep packing on the snow and keep rolling it down the hill of time, you are going to end up with a massive snowball at the end of it.

Homework

Task: Take some action today to delay your own gratification. Say no to one marshmallow today and look forward to two tomorrow.

13. F*** YOU, I WON'T DO WHAT YOU TELL ME

Nobody likes to be told what to do, least of all us entrepreneurial types. Ever since I wheel-spun out of the Civil Service office car park in my 1992 Vauxhall Cavalier with They Might Be Giants singing *"You're not the boss of me, now"* at full volume, I've designed my businesses and my life around my ultimate job description: To do what I want, when I want, how I want, where I want, if I want.

So the last thing I need is a bunch of rules, right?

I mean, I'm an entrepreneur. I'm meant to be solving problems, fighting fires and putting a dent in the universe, aren't I? Not doing the same old stuff every day. I want to be a maverick. I want every day to be different.

Good news – I'm my own boss! I can throw away the alarm clock, wear what I want to work, break for lunch when I want, work as little or as much as I want, and clock off whenever I feel like it.

Bad news – I'm my own boss! If I want to enjoy the little luxuries in life, like food in my belly and a roof over my head, I'm going to need to do some productive work.

We're going to need to find a balance here somehow.

Waking up whenever the hell you feel like it and doing whatever you want before calling it a day and hitting the golf course or the pub sounds idyllic, but it can actually paralyse you as you have that continual freedom to do anything.

When you have the freedom to choose absolutely anything you want with zero constraints, you run out of decision calories pretty damn quickly. You'll have made more than 800 decisions before you've eventually dragged your arse out of bed, washed, dressed and fed yourself.

Jocko Willink, former Navy SEAL commander and author of the excellent book *'Extreme Ownership'*, lives his life by the following mantra: Discipline = Freedom

Jocko believes that by adding in the discipline of a set routine, you actually end up with more freedom, not less. He says: "Something as simple as pre-scheduled workouts act as scaffolding around which you can more effectively plan and execute your day."

That sounds like putting the immovable objects in first to me. And who am I to argue with an ex-Navy SEAL who talks about "executing" your day?

Jocko also says: "If you want more freedom in life - be that financial freedom, more free time or even freedom from sickness and poor health - you can only achieve these things through discipline."

Once you're able to see the "rules" that discipline gives you as the scaffolding and framework upon which everything else can be built, it's easy to see how this gives you more freedom rather than less.

By blocking out time for the immovable objects and creating rules that give you the discipline to "execute" them, you move toward your goals a hundred times faster than you would if left to your own devices with complete freedom over every decision.

Things become so much easier once you get over the initial reticence of "I don't enjoy doing this", and the behaviour or action becomes automatic. Who actually enjoys brushing their teeth, tying their shoelaces or filling up with petrol? Certainly not me. You just do it without thinking about it - giving you the freedom of more time to spend on the things that you do enjoy.

Want to eat healthily? You've got a couple of options. You could employ the freedom approach and use what's left of your willpower 50 times a day to resist those doughnuts and chocolate bars, keep on walking past the fish and chips shop, and resist that quick burger at lunchtime.

Or you could use the discipline approach and prep your meals in advance for the whole week. This would give you the scaffolding upon which you can build better health, a great looking body and a longer life span. It'll make going to the gym and working out easier and it'll make resisting a takeaway on a Friday night a metaphorical piece of cake.

Discipline or diabetes. You choose.

700 ways to kill me

Scott Adams, the creator of the Dilbert cartoons, wrote in his 2013 book *'How to Fail at Almost Everything and Still Win Big'* about the secret to happiness. He studied psychology and, in particular, persuasion for several decades now, so don't dismiss him as just "a bloke who draws cartoons". He knows a thing or two about how the brain works.

Adams says: "The single biggest trick for manipulating your happiness chemistry is being able to do what you want when you want."

That sounds familiar. That's half of my ideal job description!

Now, you may think that is the polar opposite of Jocko Willink's views on discipline. But let me repeat Adams' quote with some specific emphasis: "The single biggest trick for manipulating your happiness chemistry is being able to do what you want *when* you want."

It's not the "what" that matters, it is the "when" that is the most important.

Having the freedom to eat your favourite meal is nice. But if the only time you were allowed to eat it was immediately after you'd filled up on junk food, you wouldn't be very happy, would you?

Remember Gary Halbert and his starving crowd? Any old burger or hot dog would make the starving crowd happy. But if you returned half an hour later with a plate of the finest steak cooked by a Michelin-starred chef, you wouldn't get many takers because the timing was wrong. Your once-starving crowd are now a satiated crowd.

Doesn't money make you happy? Yes, it can. Up to a point.

In his book, Adams says: "It's hard to become rich enough to buy your own private island, but, relatively speaking, it's easier to find a job with flexible hours. A person with a flexible schedule and average resources will be happier than a rich person who has everything *except* a flexible schedule. Step one in your search for happiness is to continually work toward having *control* of your schedule."

Control of your schedule and the flexibility to create your own rules. You decide what the immovable objects are going to be and, crucially, you decide *when* you're going to tackle them.

So, I'm going to bastardise Jocko Willink's mantra (please don't tell him as I'm pretty sure he could kill me in about 700 different ways) to the following:

Discipline + Flexibility = Freedom.

Discipline and flexibility are two sides of the same coin. You may think they contradict each other, but when you have the flexibility to decide what discipline to put in place, that's where true freedom comes from.

Parents of young children will know all about discipline. After the morning military regime to get them ready for school, Dad's Cabs or Mum's Motors drop the little angels off at the school gates for 8.45am with lunchbox in hand, a £1 coin for the seemingly fortnightly mufti day, and a cross-section of an active volcano made out of toilet rolls and papier-mâché.

Pick them up again at 3.15pm and ferry them to their after-school dodgeball class or guitar lessons. Then it's back home in time to help them with their homework, cook them a healthy and nutritious meal (which they'll turn their noses up at, so maybe fishfingers and waffles again), force them to have a bath, read them a story and try all manner of psychological persuasion techniques to get them to go to sleep at a reasonable hour.

Repeat this every day from Monday to Friday, every week for 39 weeks per year.

No flexibility.

But what if we removed all the discipline and had 100 per cent flexibility, giving children the opportunity to do whatever they want, whenever they want, all the time?

We already have such places. They're called soft play centres. And they're not somewhere any sane parent willingly spends more than 30 minutes a year if they can possibly help it. When one of our kids gets an invite to a birthday party at a soft play centre, Sarah and I actually draw straws.

"It's your turn. I did the last one"

"Bugger. Do I have to stay? Can't I just sit in the car outside?"

So we need that balance between discipline and flexibility. For me, that means the flexibility to decide what discipline, what immovable objects I want to put in place – and where (or more specifically, *when*) I want to put them.

In his book, Adams describes how he's particularly contented at the moment. He's sitting in a comfortable chair with his dog by his side, enjoying a nice cup of coffee (Adams that is, not the dog). He's just come from the gym, so he's feeling relaxed and in the mood to write.

"By any definition, what I'm doing is work. But because I can control the timing of it on this particular day, it doesn't feel like work. I've transformed work into pleasure simply by having control over *when* I do it."

Discipline + Flexibility = Freedom.

Freedom = Happiness.

Won't work Wednesdays?

I know what you're thinking. "But John, I thought you were all about lifestyle businesses – rejecting the 5am club, the hustle brigade, the JFDIers of this world, and drumming to your own beat? And now you're saying I should live my life by a set of rules and regulations? What if I don't want to be the next Elon Musk or Oprah Winfrey? What if I just want to work a bit less and spend more time with my family?"

Don't worry; I haven't abandoned my ambitious lifestyle business roots. Yes, I've talked about billionaires and people who have reached the very top of their game in this book. And if that's what you aspire to, then becoming a Routine Machine will get you there.

But you don't have to shoot for the Moon in order to put these principles into action.

If you want better results, you need better routines.

If you want a better lifestyle, you need better lifestyle routines.

If you want more R&R, you need more R&R routines.

If you want a better work/life balance, you need better work/life routines.

Remember, you learned earlier about your success macros? If you feel that your "me time" macro is suffering, then let's dial that up with some new "me time" routines. Block out 15 minutes a day for some meditation. Take one day off every month for a spa day. Clear your calendar every Friday afternoon or refuse to work Wednesdays and spend that time doing something you love instead such as heading to the gym, walking the dogs, getting some retail therapy, sitting and reading, or whatever *you* choose.

For me, gym time is "me time", so I block out a couple of hours twice a week, usually on the same days every week so it's programmed into the Computer. If it's 10am on a Tuesday or a Thursday, I'm probably at the gym. It's one of my immovable objects, one of the rocks that I put into my planner each week, and it takes something pretty bloody major to shift it from my diary.

If it does get moved then that's exactly what happens. It gets moved. Not cancelled. Not postponed. Moved. Because "me time" is important to me. It's one of my priorities.

Remember, my ultimate job description is to do "what I want, when I want, where I want, how I want, if I want". It's all about me and what I want. And I want "me time". I want to be healthy. I want to be full of energy and ready to take on the world. I want to live longer. I want to be stronger. I want to have a clear headspace.

That one routine (gym time twice a week) ticks all of those boxes for me, and it happens on autopilot because my Human has programmed the Computer.

Spending more time with the family is important. So I created a new routine where I don't work Friday afternoons. I start work early and finish at midday to spend a few hours with Sarah. This is quality time together, just the two of us as husband and wife, rather than Mummy and Daddy as we usually are. We can go out for lunch, watch a film or go for a walk. It's like date night, but it's a lunchtime thing. "Date lunch," perhaps?

Then at 3pm we'll pick the kids up together and do something fun as a family. We'll go bowling, have fish and chips, go rock climbing or head to the ice cream parlour.

Date lunch and then family day. What a way to end the week. I'd much rather do that than achieve inbox zero on a Friday afternoon!

We're all going on a summer holiday

Holidays are a big thing for me, too. They're a chance to relax, unwind, catch up on my reading list, spend more quality time with the family and get some sun on my back.

But back in my hustling days, holidays were a mere distraction. Sarah would moan that we hadn't had a holiday for ages and I would begrudgingly book one, but set some ground rules: "We can only go away for seven nights, the laptop has to come with us and I need to do a couple of hours of work every day."

I recall a trip to Portugal back in 2004 where I spent almost the entire holiday on the phone or on the laptop. We were going through a massive expansion, opening new offices and taking on new members of staff while I was away.

I barely got outside, let alone got a tan.

I returned to the UK more stressed than before I left, with more than 2,000 emails to sort through, all sorts of fire-fighting to be done in the new offices, and a £279 data roaming bill to boot.

I believed there was no way that the business could possibly run without me. After all, nobody can do things as well as me, can they? Well, not if you don't let them they can't.

Fast forward to the present day and my take on holidays has changed somewhat. If you want better holidays, you need better routines.

I still have rules for holidays, but they now look more like this: "We will go away for a minimum of 14 nights. The laptop will stay at home. The team, systems and processes will look after everything, and I'll work no more than a few hours per week."

Every year when I get my new year-planner whiteboard, the very first things that get written on (in bright orange pen) are the holidays. I start with all the trips that we've got booked – everything from a fortnight in the sun to a week in a cottage to a short city break. Then I'll add (in a blue pen) all the rest of the school holidays. This shows me when we could go away, but don't currently have anything booked.

Out comes the green pen next, and in goes all the "fun stuff" that's already in the diary for the year such as gigs, nights out, plays, football matches, etc.

By now, the year ahead looks bloody awesome. Nothing but holidays, potential holidays and fun stuff.

They're the rocks. They go in first.

I always book my holidays almost a year in advance and there are two reasons for this:

1. It gives me more time to earn the money to pay for them.
2. I get to look forward to the holiday for longer.

And, of course, when they're all booked a year in advance it makes planning so much easier. When I'm starting January with a new, blank planner, I can block out our trip to Tenerife in October already.

When it comes to October and I'm planning my goals for the following year, I'll include holidays that I want to book the following year, but actually take the year after that. So in 2020, I'll be setting goals for a holiday that I want to take in 2022 – that's forward thinking!

My dream holiday routine is to spend 12 weeks a year outside of the UK. But that's not really practical. Sarah's a primary school teacher and we've got two young children also at school, so we're restricted to going away during school holidays when the cost of holidays tends to treble.

I would also prefer to spend time outside of the UK during the winter when the weather's pants in this country. But, of course, the British school system front-loads holidays for the summer when the weather's better here, but too hot abroad.

Long term, though, that's the path we're on. Winters abroad, summers in the UK. We'll keep on tweaking the routine each year until we get there. We'll keep following the signposts. And I *know* we will get there.

Four hours, my arse

I read Tim Ferriss's book *'The Four-Hour Work Week'* many years ago and marvelled at the way he dealt with email. Tim claimed to only check his emails once a week. He set up an out-of-office autoresponder that said something like: "I only check email once a week. I'll get back to you on Monday. If it's urgent, call the office."

I tried it for a week. I set up the message to go out to those who emailed me and then shut down my inbox.

Then I got an instant messenger notification. "Just sent you an email and got your autoresponder. WTF?"

An hour later the phone rang. "Hi John, I've just emailed you something. Could you take a look please?"

That continued five or six times a day until Monday came around and it was time for me to blitz through these emails. I'd set aside four hours, just like Timbo had.

Inbox: 1,879 (1,868 unread).

Oh!

It took me a day and a half to clear them all. And then another half a day to deal with the replies to my (belated) reply.

Four-hour work week my arse!

So I went back to my old way of doing things, which I guess is the way most people do it – you dip in and dip out of your inbox throughout the day or maybe have it open in a separate window so that you can spot anything important that comes through and jump on it immediately.

Now, that might achieve a nice tidy inbox, but it doesn't leave you time to get much else done. One of my mentors used to say: "Your inbox is everyone else's to-do list." When you're working in your inbox, you're working on other people's priorities rather than your own.

I eventually found a happy medium between the two approaches. I'd block out time every day for my daily one thing and ensure that I achieved my weekly one thing towards the first half of the week. This would often mean ignoring my inbox for a day or two.

Let me repeat that – I'd completely ignore my inbox for a couple of days. I'd accept the chaos that would inevitably ensue as mere collateral damage. I'd then schedule in some "stuff" time midweek to catch up on all those things that I'd let slide over the previous days such as the inbox, the admin, the paperwork, and the voicemails.

And do you know what? There was no chaos. There was no catastrophe. The world didn't fall apart. I didn't lose customers hand-over-fist and not one single person complained about me taking a few days to reply.

Some of the "urgent issues" turned out not to be urgent after all and managed to resolve themselves. Ninety per cent of what was in my inbox could be deleted without further action anyway. I was just doing this in one large batch rather than dribs and drabs every single day.

After a few months of implementing this, something really interesting happened. The number of emails I received dropped dramatically. It turns out that by not immediately replying to every single person who emailed me, I was training them not to expect a same-day response. In some cases, I'd trained them not to expect a same-week response and others now knew that emailing me wouldn't get a response full-stop.

"If you want something done, ask a busy person," they say. Well, if you want something done, don't ask me. I'm busy doing my one thing.

Sorry to interrupt you...

I noticed something interesting while writing this book. In preparation to get "in the zone" and get a decent chunk of my ideas down on paper, I blocked out a week at the end of November to focus entirely on writing to the detriment of everything else.

I cleared the decks, made sure that the entire week was blocked out in my diary and let all the key people in my team know that I was going to be MIA for the whole week. I set up an out-of-office autoresponder and told anyone who "needed" me that I wasn't around that particular week, but that I'd be back in the week commencing November 26th.

I accepted that chaos would ensue and left a good-sized buffer zone for the following week to play catch-up.

Two things happened during my book-writing week. First, the people who emailed me received the "I'm not here" autoreply. Many of them replied to that autoreply, telling me not to worry about their first message as they'd sort whatever problem or question they had themselves. And those I dealt with a week later understood perfectly, were in no way offended and wished me all the best with the book.

It worked so well that I now use this routine every time I need to block out an entire day or know that it will be a few days before I get around to "stuff". I turn on my out-of-office autoresponder (even though I'm still in the office – sneaky eh?). If people think I'm not here, they're more understanding when I take four days to reply to them. The expectations have been set and those expectations have been met.

The second thing that happened during my book-writing week was that I still got interrupted. I stayed off social media until the evenings, only to find several messages from people who needed something "urgent" (like asking for a new World Domination Planner, asking where a particular invoice gets sent or getting me to sign a form). And every single one of these messages started with the following words: "Sorry to interrupt you. Hope the book writing's going well, but..."

So these were people who knew that I'd blocked out the time to do nothing but write. They knew I'd set a tough target for myself and would be really up against it. But they were still more concerned about *their* priorities and *their* to-do list than they were about mine. Which is fine. My priority is *my* priority. I don't expect it to be anyone else's.

That's normal human behaviour.

But you have to give priority to *your* priority over other people's. Once you've done *your* one thing, then you can help other people with their tasks. Fit your own oxygen mask first.

But I have a special brain...

Allegra, one of our One Percenters, has ADHD and struggles to maintain focus. She knows that routine is something that helps her and when she has forced herself to work within the discipline of a set structure, it has worked for her. But she often falls back into old habits. She said:

> *"I like the idea of it. I find that I need a really strict routine because I get distracted so easily. I did do the whole 'get up at 5.30am thing'. I did it for three weeks, but I just went back to bed at 9am. I did do 90 minutes of productive work in that time and it was good to begin with, but I was so wiped out that I gave up after three weeks.*
>
> *I saw a tweet from Inc.com saying that 'the world's most successful people get up at 4am' and JK Rowling replied, saying: 'Piss off'. That was permission enough for me to sack it off.*
>
> *For me, it needs to be tiny chunks. Although I am a big picture person, in order for me to actually get stuff done, it needs to be really simple, really straightforward and really small otherwise I just won't do it.*
>
> *If I don't have an 'I'm doing this today' list, I'll just float around doing nothing. Without that list, I have everything to do, so I get overwhelmed and do nothing. If I get lost, then I'll just do another brain dump, go through the 'could-do list' again and write a new daily plan.*
>
> *So I squeeze my brain out. Then look at what's the priority and plan that out.*

The main rule for me is that it has to be written down. If it's not there in black and white, then it won't get done. When I don't do this, I just float around 'pottering' with things that grab my attention.

I do the same as Steve Jobs and Mark Zuckerberg. I wear the same outfit – jeans, T-shirt, and a fleece every day. Not because I read some article on decision fatigue, but because it's just easier for me. There's already too much for me to decide on.

I'd like to train my brain to do what I tell it. But training is about having rules and I can't do that!

Even though I'm creating the rules, I think my brain is rebelling and saying, 'You can't tell me what to do!' I'll do the opposite. I really would cut my nose off to spite my face. Even if it's something I really wanted to do, if someone else told me to do it I'd refuse!"

It's interesting to see that the could-do list and daily planner has helped Allegra. Where she falls down is not using those tools that help her all the time, every time, without fail. She knows what works for her and she knows what she needs to do.

Sometimes she's able to tell herself to "just do it" and she'll comply. Other times, she'll rebel. The key, as Allegra says, is baby steps. The could-do list and daily planner give her the scaffolding to bolt everything else onto. So she may put something in place that helps her notice when she's starting to drift and brings her back to the brain dump. This could be as simple as a reminder on her phone, an automated daily nudge that says, "How's your daily plan going?" to check that she's doing the one simple baby step and that lines up all the other dominoes.

Keep it simple. Find what works for you. And keep doing it.

Dad's dead

Starting out with 37 pence in his pocket, Neville Wright borrowed his dad's ladder, bought himself a piece of cloth and started cleaning windows. Four decades later, he sold Kiddicare.com for £70million. And in the few short years since then, he's grown his empire to more than £100million.

Neville's a serial action-taker. He loves to do a deal and he loves to sell. He's not great at reading, though, and he struggles to focus. So he gets some help there.

Very early on in his career, Neville put a team around him who were very strong in the areas he was weak, leaving him to concentrate and go all-in on his strengths. This provided him with the scaffolding he needed to bolt on the systems and processes that were required to build a multi-million-pound company from the ground up.

He devised a rather unique way of setting up and testing these systems and processes.

Kiddicare was a family business with Neville, his wife Marilyn, daughters Joanne and Elaine, and son-in-law Scott all involved in the day-to-day running of the Peterborough-based retailer, which was eventually bought by supermarket giant Morrisons.

One day, Neville sat down with the family and announced: "We're going to play a game."

What followed wasn't your typical family game of Monopoly.

"We're going to play a game called Dad's Dead," said Neville. The rules were simple. For the rest of the working day, Neville was going to pretend to be dead.

"Dad, how much do we charge for this product?"

"No idea, love. I'm dead."

"Dad, who's the best supplier for the new buggy range?"

"Don't ask me. I'm dead."

"Dad, what's the login for the online banking?"

"Dead people don't know logins."

"Can you ask your dad to sign this form please?"

"I'm sorry, he can't sign anything at the moment. He's dead."

It sounds morbid and a little trivial, but that single day showed everyone in the team just how reliant they were on one single person. If Neville was laid up in bed with flu, he'd be a massive bottleneck. If he really did drop dead, they'd be screwed.

After playing Dad's Dead, Neville made a full recovery (rumours of his death being greatly exaggerated) and was back at the helm the very next day. The first thing he did on the day of his resurrection was to ensure new systems and processes were put into place to remove him as the potential bottleneck.

Decisions were automated up to a certain level. Documents like a staff handbook and how-to manuals were created so that all of Neville's years of knowledge and experience were available to the team without them having to have physical access to the man himself.

In short, Neville made his know-how death-proof. If he'd dropped dead at any point from then on, the business would have carried on without him seamlessly.

If you're the sort of person who hates the thought of routine, then first let me congratulate you on making it almost all the way through a book about routine. Secondly, there's a lot you can learn from someone like Neville.

If you really don't want to become a Routine Machine yourself, then you can do one (or both) of the following things:

1. Set up systems and processes to automatically handle all those routines. Play Dad's Dead to help you discover what these could be.
2. Partner up with or employ someone who is the yin to your yang. Someone who is a natural Routine Machine.

That's exactly what Neville did. Despite suffering from ADHD and dyslexia, he still managed to build a £100million-plus empire from scratch and write the bestselling book, *'The Answer is Yes, Now What is the Question?'*

I had the honour of interviewing Neville for the Ambitious. Lifestyle. Business. Podcast and we talked for well over an hour about his amazing journey. You can find a link to the recording in the resources section at the end of the book.

I've got some sad and tragic news

A common complaint I hear from people who resist the discipline of routine is: "I'm a creative person. I can't work within a rigid framework." Well, you can have routine *and* flexibility, remember? You can still be creative, even with some rules and structure in place.

Discipline + Flexibility = Freedom.

If having the freedom to express yourself creatively is important to you then you may want that framework to be a little less rigid than most people. But I would argue that you'll be more creative and perform better with some routine in place.

I grew up watching Rik Mayall and Adrian Edmondson in their hit BBC2 show *'Bottom'*, a violent slapstick comedy about two sad, lonely flatmates living together in a dank flat in Hammersmith, West London. Most storylines would revolve around Richie and/or Eddie trying to persuade a lady to have sex with them and things would often turn violent, with eye-gouging, cricket-bat-wielding and testicle-walloping particular favourites (this wasn't part of the sex, I must add. Richie and Eddie were always unsuccessful in their bedroom endeavours).

In 1993, Rik and Ade took *'Bottom'* on tour with a live stage show performed in cities all over the UK. I saw their live shows twice and it amazed me how good they were at ad-libbing, always making off-the-cuff jokes to each other, deviating from the script more than they stayed on it, and appearing to have as much fun on stage as we were in the audience.

Somewhere, I've still got the original *'Bottom Live'* on VHS. It was recorded at a theatre in Southampton and I've just watched a bit on YouTube that's had me in stitches. The entire eight-minute segment is almost entirely off-script. The fun starts when Ade delivers a line (from the script) in an overly-dramatic fashion, before milking the applause of the crowd, announcing "Alan Rickman, eat your heart out," and then gesturing for Rik to continue with the line "and, cue..."

Rik doesn't look impressed and asks: "Do you want to give me the feed line again, in front of all your friends?"

"Sorry," announces Ade. "I forgot to mention, I was actually born in Southampton!"

Cue rapturous applause.

"Oh, Eddie, Eddie, Eddie... You were BORN in SOUTHAMPTON! WOW!! Why did you ever leave?"

The banter continues for several minutes, with both actors collapsing in fits of laughter at key moments while trying to get back on track – none more so than Rik trying to deliver the line: "I've got some sad and tragic news."

Quick as a flash, Ade replies with: "You don't look very upset about it. You looked a lot sadder than that in rehearsal!"

Eventually, the two drag themselves back to the plot, which revolves (very loosely) around Eddie trying to persuade Richie to commit suicide in order to claim a £15,000 inheritance for himself.

"I've decided to kill myself," announces Richie, "because I'm so tragically in debt."

Eddie looks suitably shocked, before proclaiming: "F***ing hell! A line from the play!"

Yes, Rik and Ade broke character. Yes, they went off script.

But there *were* characters. There *was* a script.

They did rehearse. They had structure and it was that structure that made it look anarchic. It was designed that way. Breaking down the "third wall" – the invisible wall between the actors and the audience – was entirely deliberate and, dare I say, it's possible some of the spontaneous ad-libbing may have been rehearsed for the TV cameras.

Rik and Ade made a living out of looking like they were making it up as they went along. But they had structure. They had rules. They had a routine. And what a routine it was. They could deviate, ad-lib, go off-piste and see where the audience took them. But they always came back to the routine (eventually). They knew where the signposts were and could always come back to the path.

Rik and Ade were Routine Machines.

Rik Mayall died of a heart attack in 2014, depriving us of more of his true comic genius. RIP Rik.

Erm, sorry... good night!

I've seen Derren Brown's live shows several times too. He never ceases to amaze me with his ability to play mind tricks on every member of the audience (including me) and in such an entertaining way. His live shows are another level up from his TV work where he's played a live game of Russian roulette, persuaded members of the public to rob a bank and convinced one teacher from Buckinghamshire that a meteor had hit the Earth, resulting in a zombie apocalypse.

A few years back, I was watching him perform a live show in the glitzy surroundings of the Plymouth Pavilions (Devon's answer to Las Vegas...if Las Vegas just consisted of a 1,500-seat auditorium that doubles up as a basketball court and an ice rink). As usual, Derren was on top form, persuading some of my fellow audience members to stick needles in their hand, chew on broken glass and stroke tarantulas.

As the show built towards its climax, Derren made a big joke about fake psychics and how they could claim to read someone's mind to get their phone number: "I'm getting a zero...seven. Anyone's number start with 07?" (For those outside of the UK, all mobile phone numbers in this country start with 07).

"...8...Yes madam... what's your number?"

"07855 123456."

Bow and take the applause.

Throughout the evening, Derren had been writing different numbers down as various scenarios played out. One person was picked at random using a Frisbee and Derren would guess what number house they lived at when they were a child. Then he'd work out how long a couple had been married and how many pets another lady had.

All this built up to a finale where Derren got members of the audience to call out some of these numbers. He wrote them all down on a massive whiteboard and asked one man to stand up.

“Janet lived at number 84, Andy and Donna have been married for 17 years, Lloyd was 15 when he lost his virginity (allegedly), Karen has 21 pets (and no life),” Derren throws out one final Frisbee and says: “Sir, what’s your name?”

“Bob”

“Bob, what number seat are you sat in?”

“310”

“So if we multiply Janet’s house by Andy and Donna’s marriage, by Lloyd’s virginity, by Karen’s pets, by Bob’s seat number, we get 65,432,155,870.”

“And if we read that number backwards, it’s 07855 123456. Bob, that’s your phone number, isn’t it?”

“No.”

“Sorry, what? That is your number, isn’t it? 07855 123456?”

“No, that’s nothing like my number.”

“Oh! Erm.. sorry! Goodnight!”

Cue disbelieving, polite applause from the audience as Derren practically ran off the stage. I thought that it was all part of the show as several of Derren’s “tricks” appear to go wrong before he reveals that was the plan all along.

Not this time.

Derren would later explain in a 2018 newspaper interview: “That was the very last moment of the show, the climax of this recurring theme we’d had for two hours, the cue for all the confetti to go off. And I was just wrong. The audience was confused. I had nothing.”

He had nothing. No structure. No rules for “what happens if it goes wrong?” No routine to fall back on. He’s never needed one before. He’d performed the same trick (the same routine) hundreds of times before and it had worked every time.

But that time it didn't. He got the maths wrong. Live on stage in front of 1,500 people.

I bet he's got a back-up finale routine now.

Homework

Task: Play a game of Dad's Dead and identify the places where you are a bottleneck. Set up new routines, systems and processes to eliminate them.

Question: What's one thing you can change in your current routine(s) to give you more discipline *and* flexibility?

Question: What rule(s) can you put in place to prevent interruptions?

14. WHAT ARE YOU GOING TO DO?

Let's pretend time travel is possible and you can take a short hop back just five years. If you could travel five years into the past and change just one thing about your life then, what would it be?

Returning to the present, what effect would that one change have made to your current life?

Where would you be right now if you'd started five years ago? What kind of person would you be now as a result of that one change?

We've all heard of the butterfly effect – where one tiny change to the space/time continuum can have a massive impact, such as the flap of a butterfly's wings in Mexico causing a hurricane in China.

Well, you can't travel in time. You can't affect the past. But you can alter the future. Five years from now, you'll wish you started today. Flap your wings.

All these things I've done

The following is a short(ish) list of some of the routines and habits that I've started, stopped, improved and iterated over the last few years.

I've added this list to spark some ideas in your head of things that you might like to try. Please don't copy me though. This is my list of things that have worked for me. It's *not* a to-do list for you to work through.

Don't copy me.

Don't copy your friends.

Don't copy a "guru".

Find what works for you.

Tom loves to lift weights. Dave prefers playing squash. Jo is a vegan. Craig swears that grass-fed beef is a superfood. Victor knows that LinkedIn is the best place to market your business, but Mike thinks it's Facebook and Mark would rather send direct mail. If you want to get rich, Siam will tell you to invest in Cryptocurrency. Geoff will say you need a pension. James likes commercial property, while Angelos prefers buy-to-let. Shan will tell you to invest in the stock market via funds and Graham will advise you to store your wealth in fine art, wine and classic cars.

So, there's no right way. There's no wrong way.

There's only *your* way.

Here's mine. Here are 32 of the hundreds and hundreds of routines that I've adopted, adapted, improved and iterated over the last few years:

- Giving up smoking.
- Giving up alcohol.
- Giving up caffeine.
- Giving up dairy.
- Drinking three litres of water every day.
- Reintroducing caffeine.
- Reintroducing dairy.
- Going to the gym twice a week.
- Going to the gym five times a week.
- Having a daily sauna.
- Switching to natural, chemical-free toiletries.
- Replacing my car radio with audiobooks and podcasts.
- Walking 10,000 steps every day.

- Drinking fruit and vegetable juice.
- Making Friday afternoons "family day".
- Adding butter to my morning coffee.
- Sending newsletters out to clients every three months.
- Having a daily meditation practice.
- Doing some marketing every day.
- Writing weekly emails.
- Getting 8.5 hours sleep every night.
- Weekly golf coaching.
- Monthly mastermind meetings with my mentors.
- Quarterly investment reviews.
- Digital detox on every family holiday.
- Working ON the business every day.
- Keeping a food diary.
- Sleeping with earplugs in (sorry? What? I can't hear you!).
- Recording a monthly podcast.
- Time blocking and batching.
- Taking daily vitamins.
- Working in 90-day blocks.

This is your last piece of homework

This is it. The end *is in sight.*

Are you going to be one of those people who turns over the final page of this book and then almost immediately picks up the next one? The frog sitting in the corner of the library calling out: "Reddit! Reddit! Reddit!"

Or are you the sort of person who has a debrief routine every time you read a book? The sort of person who makes the decision to try at least one idea from the book, implement one change or at the very least to write down your biggest takeaway from the last few hundred pages?

You've invested several hours of your time reading this book and I truly thank you for that. But if nothing changes as a result, what was the point?

Your final piece of homework is to set up a debrief routine every time you read a book – starting with this one.

Caleb Maddix is 17 years old. He made his first million dollars aged just 15. When he was seven years old, Caleb asked his dad for some pocket money for doing chores around the house.

His dad refused, instead offering to pay Caleb $20 for every personal development book he read. The only catch was that he had to write a report on every single one – a few hundred words with the key lessons, main takeaways and action points. That's it.

If a seven-year-old kid can use this one single routine (snowballed over ten years) to make a million dollars, then why can't you?

Task: Do a full debrief of Routine Machine. Write down the key things you remember, your main takeaways, any ideas you want to try, something you're going to implement and what's *actually going to change as a result of you reading this book*. For extra brownie points, start the free 30-day challenge, join the Routine Machines Facebook group, and post your new routines for all your fellow Routine Machines to see, and to help you achieve it - full details on the next page.

15. THE NEXT 30 DAYS

Remember, there is no magic, one-size-fits-all number of days that it takes to establish a new routine - "It will take... as long as it will take!" (Thank you Mr. Bull).

However, most people struggle with the first couple of weeks. They race out of the starting blocks on day one, full of motivation and best intentions. Day two, and they're still very focused and aware of the routine change, and giving themselves a virtual pat on the back.

A week-and-a-half in though, and their automatic script (created years ago by the Monkey) finds them sat in a fast-food restaurant because they were short on time, or skipping a workout because it's raining, or the world's most frequently-used excuse:

Life got in the way.

Because life will get in the way - I can guarantee it. As the famous philosopher Mike Tyson once said "Everyone has a plan until they get punched in the mouth." You will get punched in the mouth by life. You'll get winded. You'll get knocked down. Again, and again. But will you get up and start swinging again, or will you get counted out?

Sticking with the boxing metaphors, you've probably heard the following quote from fictional boxer Rocky Balboa before:

> *"Let me tell you something you already know. The world ain't all sunshine and rainbows. It's a very mean and nasty place and I don't care how tough you are, it will beat you to your knees and keep you there permanently if you let it. You, me, or nobody is gonna hit as hard as life. But it ain't about how hard ya hit. It's about how hard you can get hit and*

keep moving forward. How much you can take and keep moving forward. That's how winning is done!"

Yep, Rocky Balboa was a Routine Machine.

You can't have Rocky in your corner as you become a Routine Machine, but you can have me.

I'll be there for you. Me, and hundreds of your fellow Routine Machines. All cheering you on from the sidelines - willing you to succeed, and helping you when life hits you hard.

That's why I've created a free 30-day challenge to accompany this book - you'll get to meet your fellow Routine Machines, reinforce everything you've learnt over the last few hundred pages, and get a daily bit of bonus content from me personally, showing you how you can keep being a Routine Machine, long after you've put this book down.

When life hits you hard, and the Monkey starts to wrestle control of the Computer from you again, you'll be ready for it - because you're a Routine Machine, and "that's how winning is done!"

Are you ready for the challenge? Start your 30-day journey at:

- www.routinemachine.co.uk/challenge

16. START NOW

The routine doesn't matter. What matters is that you have a routine.

- Start by doing one push-up
- Start by drinking one cup of water
- Start by reading one page
- Start by walking one lap
- Start by writing one paragraph
- Start by attending one event
- Start by meditating for one minute
- Start by asking for one sale
- Start by saving one pound
- Start by smiling at one person
- Start by changing one thing
- Start today
- Repeat tomorrow

That's how Routine Machines are built.

WHAT'S NEXT?

Thank you so much for investing your time in reading this book. It has been a pleasure sharing my work with you. I hope it's triggered some inspiration, got the cogs turning in your head, and encouraged you to think about how you could improve and iterate your current routines.

I'd love to hear from you if this book has resonated with you in any way. Send me an email at john@bigidea.co.uk and let me know what you're going to change (or have already).

If you're looking for something to read next, allow me to offer a suggestion. If you've enjoyed reading Routine Machine then you may well enjoy my other writing as well. As mentioned, I send out free weekly articles every Wednesday lunchtime to my email subscribers. You can get these at my website:

- www.bigidea.co.uk

Subscribers are also the first to hear about new podcast episodes, my latest books and also have access to my recommended reading list – a comprehensive list of more than 80 must-read books that I've hand-picked, covering a wide range of topics, such as sales and marketing, productivity, health, relationships, mindset, customer service, financial, investment and motivation, as well as inspirational biographies and autobiographies.

You can download my recommended reading list from www.bigidea.co.uk, where you will also find links to our Ambitious. Lifestyle. Business. Podcast, as well as details about our One Percent Club and how to join the waiting list.

RESOURCES

You can download all the resources mentioned in this book at www.routinemachine.co.uk , including:

- My World Domination Planner
- My interview by The ONE Thing podcast
- My 30/60/90-day average spreadsheet
- My interview with Neville Wright
- An hour-long Routine Masterclass video from me
- Examples of my weekly emails
- The one sheet of A4 that 10x'ed my business
- A compound interest calculator
- More help with stacking up one per cent gains
- Some ideas on other books you might like to read next
- The link to my Ambitious.Lifestyle.Business. Facebook group

ABOUT THE AUTHOR

John Lamerton is a serial entrepreneur and investor. He is a former civil servant, who started a dotcom company back in 2000 despite having no skills, knowledge or experience – "But then, neither did most of the other dotcom businesses at that time, so I was in good company!"

He's owned a website that told students where to get free sachets of shampoo, one that told people they'd been caught speeding (when they hadn't), and one that told football fans where to get the best pies.

Before he knew it, he was running a dating website, selling office space, working with florists to sell online, and selling package holidays to the Algarve. He's also owned a bingo website, a finance blog, sold mobile phone insurance, and streamed live sports events.

Trust me, that's the short version. John's owned and operated more than 100 different websites since that first one in 2000. Most have been either sold or closed down and he now works primarily in three sectors:

Sports betting: John owns a number of online sports betting brands and specialises in building large, loyal communities of sports betting fans. He's always looking to add to his portfolio, so if you know of any sports betting communities that are looking for a new home, please get in touch via john@bigidea.co.uk.

Mentoring: John's main passion these days is mentoring ambitious lifestyle business owners. John runs a paid group mentoring programme (the One Percent Club), as well as a FREE Facebook group, details of which can be found at:

- www.bigidea.co.uk.

Investing: John is an angel investor to some of his mentoring clients. He also buys large, established websites, particularly in the sports betting sector.

John is also a perennial optimist, firmly believing that the mighty Plymouth Argyle will one day play in the top-tier of English football. So far though, he's witnessed four promotions and six relegations. Still, it only takes a couple of back-to-back promotions...

He lives in Plymouth with his wife Sarah and two children, Jack and Harry.

He's also a bit of a fanboy of Warren Buffett.

And he can always, ALWAYS be bribed with cake.

Mmm, cake...

BIBLIOGRAPHY

Adams, S. (2013). *How to Fail at Almost Everything and Still Win Big: Kind of the Story of My Life.* Portfolio Penguin.

Agassi, A. (2010). *Open: An Autobiography.* HarperCollins.

Catalano, F., & Smith, B. (2000). *Internet Marketing for Dummies.* New York: John Wiley & Sons.

Craig, A. (2015). *How to Own the World: A Plain English Guide to Thinking Globally and Investing Wisely.* CreateSpace Independent Publishing Platform.

Elrold, H. (2017). *The Miracle Morning: The 6 Habits That Will Transform Your Life Before 8AM.* John Murray Learning.

Ferriss, T. (2011). *The 4-Hour Work Week: Escape the 9-5, Live Anywhere and Join the New Rich.* Vermilion.

Frankl, V. (2004). *Man's Search For Meaning: The classic tribute to hope from the Holocaust.* Rider.

Gerber, M. (1995). *The E-Myth Revisited: Why Most Small Businesses Don't Work and What to Do About It.* Picnic Time.

Jervis, N. (2017). *Law Firm Growth Formula: How smart solicitors attract more of the right clients at the right price to grow their law firm quickly.* Rethink Press.

Keller, G., & Papasan, J. (2014). *The ONE Thing: The Surprisingly Simple Truth Behind Extraordinary Results.* London: John Murray Learning.

King, S. (2012). *On Writing: A Memoir of the Craft.* Hodder Paperbacks.

Kiyosaki, R. T. (2011). *Rich Dad Poor Dad: What the Rich Teach Their Kids About Money That the Poor and Middle Class Do Not!* Plata Publishing.

Lamerton, J. (2017). *Big Ideas... For Small Businesses: Simple, Practical Tools and Tactics to Help Your Small Business Grow.* Let's Tell Your Story Publishing.

Peters, P. S. (2012). *The Chimp Paradox: The Mind Management Programme to Help You Achieve Success, Confidence and Happiness.* London: Vermilion.

Reynolds, G. (2013). *The First 20 Minutes: Surprising Science Reveals How We Can Exercise Better, Train Smarter, Live Longer.* Avery Publishing Group.

Sinek, S. (2011). *Start With Why: How Great Leaders Inspire Everyone To Take Action.* Penguin.

Vale, J. (2011). *Kick The Drink...Easily.* Carmarthen: Crown House Publishing.

Walker, M. (2017). *Why We Sleep: The New Science of Sleep and Dreams.* Allen Lane.

Willink, J., & Babin, L. (2017). *Extreme Ownership: How U.S. Navy SEALs Lead and Win.* St. Martin's Press.

Wright, N. (2016). *The Answer is Yes Now What is the Question?* Upfront Publishing.

Made in United States
Orlando, FL
27 September 2022

22831886R00153